THE SASQUATCH IN MINNESOTA

REVISED EDITION

MIKE QUAST

UNTOLD PUBLISHING

To report Bigfoot encounters in Minnesota or for further information the author may be contacted at mqstk@aol.com.

Cover design by Doug Hajicek.
Copyright 2021

INTRODUCTION - 10 YEARS SEEKING SASQUATCH

Why am I writing this book?

I could just as easily ask- What is it that makes a perfectly sane human being dedicate a large part of his life to pursuing something so elusive that most people do not even believe it exists?

What causes someone to spend enormous amounts of time and money (which could probably be better spent) in an endeavor that is both physically and mentally demanding and exposes him to great ridicule, all the while having only the very tiniest chance of success?

I have been doing it for a decade now, and I still don't know.

In 1990, I published "The Sasquatch in Minnesota," following it in 1991 with "Creatures of the North: The New Minnesota Sasquatch Encounters." In one way, these were just two more additions to the large collection of books dealing with the subject of giant, hairy manlike/apelike creatures that reportedly exist in our wilderness areas. But in another, more personal way, they told an important piece of my life story.

On a warm, sunny summer day in 1976, I was with my family on a leisurely drive through the area of Strawberry Lake, located near the Indian community of White Earth in western Minnesota. I was just eight years old and was enjoying the view as we drove through the forested countryside, hoping to catch sight of a deer or other animal.

Suddenly I did see something. Standing between 75 and 100 yards ahead of the car, on the left side of the road, was a dark black object about 6 1/2 or seven feet tall. At first, I thought it was a burned, blackened tree trunk, but that notion quickly went out the window when it stepped away from the road and walked on two legs into the woods, disappearing from view. No one else in the car had seen it, so I alone was left to wonder- what was it?

A man? Not likely, owing to its color and large size.

A bear? Even less likely, since although bears can stand and even take a few clumsy steps on their hind legs, they always drop down to all fours to go anywhere.

There was really only one other option I could think of. I believed then, as I do now, that I'd seen a sasquatch, or "Bigfoot," one of those legendary giant man-apes said to roam the wild places of North America. From that moment on, I have been determined to learn more about these creatures, and the more one learns, the more curious one becomes.

It was in 1987 that I began to seriously investigate this phenomenon, and I learned quickly that for some reason, it is a subject that stirs great emotion in people. The sasquatch is regarded by many as a big joke, a silly piece of folklore that somehow became popular, not as a real animal at all. Therefore, are those of us who have actually seen one in the flesh included in the joke? If so, we are not laughing.

Most of the general public is still completely unaware of the scope of this phenomenon and of the number of investigators in the United States and Canada who pursue it. And what is my role?

Through what feels to me to have been a minimal effort on my part, I have somehow become the chief investigator for the state of Minnesota.

Of course, this is just a fancy way of saying that I'm about the only person who's really gotten out there and done the work on a large scale.

So, I ask again - why am I writing this third book?

Two reasons, one of which is the very work I've been doing for the past decade. I've made a lot of observations and formed many opinions in that time, and in this my ten-year anniversary, it seemed fitting to share some of them. The other reason is the state of Minnesota, my home. Look up this state in other books on "Bigfoot", and you will probably find less than a dozen reports listed for all of recorded history. This was discouraging at first, but as I did not have the resources to go to the more popular Pacific Northwest or some other "hot spot" for any length of time to conduct research, and since after all, I had seen a sasquatch myself in Minnesota, it was here that I established myself. And as I soon discovered, the other books are quite incomplete.

A good number of reports have come to my attention since the publication of my last book. My Minnesota file now contains over 130 of them, a fact I am quite proud of. Some of these have been published in newspapers but never widely circulated, while others were completely unknown until I came across them. A small percentage are my own personal experiences (my 1976 sighting, various footprint discoveries, etc.), but most are not, and I take credit for assembling them into the collection you'll see here.

But isn't this kind of book dreadfully monotonous? We've seen it over and over - books that simply tell story after story, sighting after sighting, footprint after footprint. It was a new idea once, but we've gotten very used to it. So why do it one more time? Because I am very serious about getting this information out there, establishing Minnesota as what I feel it is- one of the best-suited states east of the Rockies to shelter these giant creatures (and I do like to fancy myself a fairly decent writer, so hopefully my telling of the tale will keep you entertained).

MINNESOTA- The Gopher State. Land of 10,000 Lakes. It is a state with many vastly different features. It contains the Twin Cities of Minneapolis and St. Paul (a major metropolitan area by anyone's standards). It is an industry leader in agriculture, shipping, yard iron ore production. Yet, it also has thousands of square miles of unspoiled wilderness throughout its wide expanse. An analysis of the land reveals the following statistics:

Crops: 44%
Forest: 34%
Pasture: 11%
Water: 6%
Wetlands: 3%
Mines: 0.1%

This leaves only 1.9% for cities.

With all of its lakes, actually numbering close to 15,000, Minnesota has more shoreline than Hawaii, California, and Florida combined, and these lakes are filled with many kinds of fish from the huge muskie to the tiny shiner minnow. In the woods, one may find such animals as white-tailed deer, moose, black bear, timber wolf, lynx, and bobcat. Even the elusive mountain lion still prowls here, though it's hard to convince the "experts" of that. Bird watchers love it here as well, enjoying glimpses of the rare bald eagle and listening to the crazy call of the loon, our state bird.

The Norway Pine is Minnesota's state tree, but overall, the forests here are mostly mixed growth, with both deciduous and coniferous trees. A perfect habitat for the sasquatch.

A spokesman for the state DNR (Department of Natural Resources) stated to me in a letter that "...most bigfoot-type observations occur in the Pacific Northwest. If such a creature really exists, it is not unreasonable to expect that one could stray into Minnesota." However, such authorities have put forth very little effort to study the situation. In fact, hardly anyone has. But there are a few people besides myself who have worked at it to some degree in Minnesota.

During the late 1970s and early 1980s, a Mr. Donald Peterson of Litchfield was active in investigations, allied with an Iowa sasquatch tracker named Cliff Labreque.

Also, at that time, two teenagers, Ted Steiner and David Warner were publishing a small newsletter called "Minnesota Bigfoot News" and operated a "Bigfoot Center" in the basement of Warner's home in Edina.

A Richard Johnson of St. Paul searched for the creatures in northern Minnesota in 1978-79 and claimed a sighting (details in chapter three).

Although I've attempted to contact these people, I have been unsuccessful. I have been in touch, however, with Mark A. Hall and Tim Olson.

Hall is a Fortean researcher (interested in all manner of strange phenomena) in Bloomington, a suburb of the Twin Cities. A colleague of popular writer Loren Coleman, he has an extensive library and has written a number of books and articles of his own. Mark is probably best known as the foremost authority on thunderbirds, giant birds of prey that are said to inhabit North America, but his interest in manlike beasts also runs very deep. He has been outspoken in his belief in what he calls the "true giants," creatures that may exceed 15 feet in height, not a popular belief by any means but one he treats with true scholarly wisdom. However, he is employed by the federal government, and most of his time is spent making a living (a problem for all of us in this field- there is no money whatsoever in sasquatch chasing); thus, he rarely gets out into the field. He is a virtual human storehouse of information, however, and has helped me a lot.

Tim Olson is younger and more active on the physical end of things. He has been my partner on and off for several years since Mark Hall first introduced us (they were neighbors), but though he is a Minnesota native, he now lives in northern California, where the name "Bigfoot" first arose. He has been allied at various times with such well-known investigators as Rich Grumley of the now-defunct California Bigfoot Organization and Warren Thompson and Arch Buckley of the Bay Area Group.

When I met Tim, I had recently begun publishing a monthly newsletter, *The Sasquatch Report.* He soon became my associate editor.

Since then, the project has gone in various directions, but all in all, I'd say we've done a pretty good job. I have a lot of respect for Tim;

he has to live with a medical condition that denies him many things most people take for granted, but he has a very strong religious faith, and it's gotten him through a lot of hard times.

And since late 1990, there has been Ed Trimble. "Old Ed" has been extremely valuable to me as an investigator since his own first discovery of strange tracks on his property, and many of the reports in this book were first uncovered by him. Much more on him later.

It is through the work of people like these, as well as myself that the true picture of the sasquatch's role as a member of Minnesota's fauna has emerged. And as I said, in a decade of investigating that role as well as being involved in the sasquatch field on a wider scale, I've formed my own unique set of views about the whole thing. I'd like to share some of those with you now and tell you a bit more of my story.

THE SASQUATCH REPORT AND PETER BYRNE

My newsletter, *The Sasquatch Report* (SR), is one of several such publications within the field right now. However, as far as I know, only the *Bigfoot Co-Op* out of Whittier, California, surpasses it in its longevity. What's more, it is monthly, whereas the Co-Op is bimonthly and has sometimes disappeared for months at a time, the SR no matter what else can be said about it, it does seem to have staying power. And here is how it came about:

In October of 1989, I traveled by Greyhound to Hood River, Oregon, to meet with famed "Bigfoot" hunter Peter Byrne. I had been corresponding with him for some time, choosing him mainly because of an information packet he'd sent me when I was a child. That had been back in the 1970s when his Bigfoot Information Center was operating, and he'd been publishing the monthly newsletter, *Bigfoot News*. There were other investigators I could have contacted, but having him fresh in my memory made me choose him.

I stayed with Peter, his wife Celia, and their five-year-old daughter Rara overnight, finding their home along the Hood River to be comfortable and gracious. (Incidentally, I found it impressive that a man could have his first child at the age of 58.)

Rara was a little bundle of energy. Celia ("Dede" to her friends) seemed even more into conservation than her famous husband and had been live-trapping mice in the house to release them outside.

Peter said he had retired from the Bigfoot business in 1979 because he had simply "had enough." After a lifetime of thrilling adventures- big game hunting in Nepal, yeti expeditions in the high Himalayas, white water rafting excursions, then on the conservation movement and the founding of a tiger preserve, along with the Bigfoot quest- he seemed content now to take it easy in his picturesque mountain surroundings. Beautiful Mount Hood loomed on the horizon from the end of his driveway.

During the day, we visited Fermin Osborne, a retired logger who had had a famous creature sighting along with two other men in 1974.

"I looked over and saw this big old monster," he said matter-of-factly as he told the story.

Then at night, Peter and I sat by his fireplace listening to opera, sipping hot rum, and talking about the sasquatch. The surroundings, plus his suave Irish accent, seemed to lend a distinct air of class to the whole business.

Before I had to catch the bus home the next morning, Peter showed me one of the few remaining complete sets of *Bigfoot News*, 57 issues dated Oct. '74-June '79. I had talked about how I had been thinking of starting a newsletter, and in a surprising act of generosity, he gave me the complete set, said I could use anything from it that I wished, and suggested I even use the *Bigfoot News* title and logo.

It was a few months before I got everything organized. In spreading the word about my intentions, I learned that Don Keating of Newcomerstown, Ohio already had a newsletter called *Bigfoot News* and wasn't about to let me use that name, so I changed it to *The Sasquatch Report*, which began in April 1990 and endures to this day without a single month missed and never late by more than a few days.

I did use one major thing from Peter's publication- its four-page format. This made it easy to print on one single 11" x 17" sheet of paper. Only a few times has an extra page been inserted.

Things change, of course. That's part of what defines life. Events involving Peter Byrne since then are now a matter of record, fully documented elsewhere, and I won't rehash things too much.

Peter's retirement did not last forever. Shortly after my visit, he was off to Nepal again to work on an elephant study project, resulting in the book and t.v. special "Tula Hatti, the Last Great Elephant." And not long after that, his 1970s benefactor, Boston's Academy of Applied Science (best known for their Loch Ness Monster research), decided to fund him for a new 5-year sasquatch hunt. And thus was born the Bigfoot Research Project. It was a big operation, with computers and motion sensors and all manner of other high-tech gear. Peter's critics asserted that it was primarily a giant publicity gimmick, as they had said of his earlier efforts. At this point, I honestly don't know the truth about Peter Byrne, nor do I really care as it does not affect my own work in Minnesota in any way. The Bigfoot Research Project did provide funding for my newsletter for a time, as they did for others around the country, but that too is open to interpretation as to motive by Peter's critics.

But my publishing endeavors suddenly put me in the midst of a scandal that became known as the "Great Footprint Caper." To make a long story short, it involved a photo of a sasquatch track circulated by Peter and an assertion that it was that of the creature in the famous 1967 Patterson film from Bluff Creek, California, found seven years prior to the filming. Others, however, including investigator John Green in British Columbia (who had considerable experience with tracks from Bluff Creek), were quick to point out that it was most definitely not the same, and that in fact, Peter had published the exact same photo years before with a completely different story as to date, location, and track dimensions.

Byrne and Green debated angrily back and forth in the pages of The Sasquatch Report for four months until I finally gave up on the whole issue and said, "Enough." After all, how could this possibly serve to help find a live sasquatch now, a quarter-century after the fact, no matter where the track came from?

It seems to have been this issue and other disagreements between him and Green that estranged me from Peter Byrne, who was very angry that I wouldn't take his side exclusively. Of course, I didn't take anyone else's either, but so be it. People are funny.

MORE SASQUATCH SCANDAL

We sasquatch investigators are a curious lot. We are not scientists unless you consider cryptozoology (the study of "hidden" animals) to be an amateur science. Rather, we are pretty much all private working citizens who pursue our quarry in our spare time on shoestring budgets. We like to make little corners of our homes into offices, put maps on the wall with multiple-colored pins sticking in them, and try to appear as official as possible. Many of us also like to form organizations or "information centers" and have business cards and stationery printed. (I myself once tried to form a group, the short-lived Minnesota Bigfoot/Sasquatch Organization.)

As stated before, a fair number of publications resulted from all this as well.

It's all very impressive, to be sure, and maybe someday it'll all be worth it.

I would like to call all of these people a real functioning "network" of investigators. I really would. Unfortunately, that is just not the case. In this field, everyone is well-meaning, and almost everyone believes the sasquatch is real, but somehow no one agrees on anything else. Just believing is not enough. You must believe for the right reasons, and your motives must be like everyone else's. If not, no matter how nice a guy you might be, you automatically make enemies. As I said, this subject is highly emotional.

I have ended up in more than my fair share of arguments with some of these people in the past decade. Without naming names, the state of Ohio seems to be a hotbed of disagreement in sasquatch-related matters of all sorts. Newcomers to the field, especially, are often looked down upon, especially if they happen to come up with impressive evidence with a minimum of effort (which is only due to extreme luck in most cases). And if you happen to operate a newsletter and make it an open forum for people to speak their minds, watch out.

I have tried to make *The Sasquatch Report* impartial. Most issues do contain an editorial, but all contain a disclaimer that reads, "Opinions expressed by others in this newsletter are not necessarily shared or supported by the editors." But that's not enough, it seems. Over and over, people submitting their views to SR have insisted that I support them and that I refuse to print viewpoints opposing them. Usually, the cases in question are ones that I have very little or no personal opinion on anyway.

I like to use the following analogy: If some fascist dictator gives a speech and angrily insults the United States, does our media condone his views simply by reporting what he said? Of course not!

But the fact that he said it is news, like it or not. Why people refuse to let me and SR approach the sasquatch field from this standpoint is completely beyond me.

It has always been my contention that the only way the sasquatch is going to be proven real is by long, hard hours spent out in the wilderness physically searching for it, not through anything that takes place on the printed page or in a lecture hall. Spreading the word is important, surely, but in the end, it will only serve as support for more physical activity. Arguing for years over whether or not the Blue Mountains "dermal ridge tracks" are real or fake, or whether this film or that film shows a real sasquatch or a man in a costume, is completely pointless. (Films, especially, are pointless to debate unless they are of good enough quality to serve as final proof. If they're not, it doesn't matter if they're real or fake!)

I suppose it was inevitable, though, that big egos and basic human nature would cause this sad state of affairs. Yet somehow, things do occasionally get accomplished in this field. While the various cliques argue back and forth, investigations are launched. Discoveries are made. And some day, one of us is going to prove to the world once and for all that the sasquatch really exists and vindicate us all, friends and enemies alike.

And so, this book tells the story of my own investigations in my home state of Minnesota. I do not claim to be absolutely correct about everything you will read here, for I am only human and therefore imperfect and fallible, but I hope the weight of the evidence here will make at least somewhat of an impression.

This book is essentially an updated combination of my first two, with many updates, corrections, and much new information. I have also included a section this time on the neighboring states of North and South Dakota, where the sasquatch has also roamed.

A note about witnesses: In cases where the witnesses' names have not been previously published, only initials will be used unless permission has been given to use the full name.

And a note on the word "Bigfoot." It is actually a local northern California name for the creatures that simply caught on in the rest of the country through media coverage in the late 1950s, and I have always thought it sounded much too cartoon-like for a real animal; thus, I prefer to use the term "sasquatch."

Every report that I am personally aware of at this time for Minnesota and the Dakotas is included here. Many are of a more-or-less conventional nature (man sees sasquatch, sasquatch runs away) while others are downright bizarre, but all are true to the best of my knowledge, and I believe they prove the existence of the beast I saw along that forest highway all those years ago.

Author's view of Strawberry Lake sasquatch, summer 1976.

Map showing the distribution of known Minnesota sasquatch reports from 1898 to the present. Some dots represent more than one report in a single location. Stars indicate large concentrations of reports. Open circles indicate hoaxes. The arrow points to the scene of the author's own 1976 sighting.

PART I

AN OVERVIEW OF THE SASQUATCH IN MINNESOTA

1

INDIAN LEGENDS - MYTH OR REALITY?

A s it does in many other areas, the beginning of Minnesota's sasquatch saga rests with the Indians. Although they are a minority today and sometimes suffer because of it, the Indians are very much a part of the state's history. The two main tribes are the Chippewa, or Ojibwa, and the Dakota Sioux. Many of them have now become modernized and are forgetting the old ways, but a few still retain their ancient beliefs and traditions and live by codes that white men will forever be at a loss to understand.

White men first arrived in Minnesota around 1660, mainly fur trappers and explorers. They found that the Indians had a wide range of beliefs in various legendary forest creatures, including those which would later be termed "sasquatch." (This word, by the way, is not exactly of straight Indian origin as is commonly believed but was coined by J.W. Burns, a teacher in British Columbia, who created it by combining several similar-sounding Indian names for the creatures; it means, roughly, "wild man of the woods.")

Ojibwa tribes had legends about a being they called *memegwicio*, or "man of the wilderness." This was said to be about the size of a 12-year-old child by some accounts, being completely covered with hair and having a flat nose. After seeing pictures in white mens' books, some tribes said the creatures greatly resembled monkeys but were also part man.

An old legend states that Anishinabe, the Ojibwes' name for the first man, in his travels met Memegwicio, who was angered and said he knew that man would ruin the wilderness.

An intriguing story is found in the book "Haunted Heartland" by Beth Scott and Michael Norman. It is a collection of true ghost stories, but one in particular just may relate to a more physical creature that appeared to the Mandan Indians around Roseau in northwestern Minnesota.

The Windego (or Windigo, Wendigo, Wittiko, and other variations) appears frequently in the legends of northern tribes in both the United States and Canada. Some stories describe it as a hideous cannibal giant that preys upon men. Others say it is a spirit that appears as an omen of impending death, as in this one.

Sam Mickinock and his family were Mandans living near Roseau.

One day in 1898, Sam's elderly mother-in-law became ill. After three days, she got out of bed and asked to be helped into the yard. There she sat in a chair in the warm sun in the company of her granddaughter Anna and three white women who lived nearby.

Suddenly, as the story goes, the sky darkened, and the air grew cold. Anna stood and pointed out across a field. "Grandma die soon," she said. "See Windego."

All present saw a tall, white figure walking along a wooded ridge some distance away. The old woman died the following morning.

The following year Sam Mickinock and his wife were on a hunting trip across the border in Canada. While there, Mrs. Mickinock suddenly felt ill, and the couple returned to Roseau. Three days later, a neighbor, Jake Nelson, whose mother and sister had been present at the first sighting of the Windego, was alone in the Mickinocks' yard when he saw, almost in the same spot as before, another strange white figure. It appeared to stand 15 feet tall and was striding along the edge of a swamp. It then started to run, stumbling several times, and was lost from sight after about a quarter-mile. Mrs. Mickinock died the next morning.

On the first day of spring in 1904, the Windego appeared again, this time to Jake's children Jesse and Edna. They nearly ran into it as they walked to school that morning, later describing it as a giant, white all over, with a bright star in the middle of its forehead. They ran from it in fear, and three days later, a young Indian brave died for no apparent reason in the nearby village of Ross.

The same children saw the creature yet again a month later, this time on their way home from school. Again there was a sudden death.

The Windego has often been associated with tales of the sasquatch. If the thing seen in these cases was not actually something supernatural (and it did not really do anything that should make one think that it was), then there is little it could have been but a white-haired sasquatch (and at 15 feet, an enormous one- one of Mark Hall's "true giants"). The "bright star" on its forehead described by the children could have been a lighter patch in some darker hair, or it could have been light reflecting in the creature's eyes. Since the cases are so old, there is no way to be sure.

It's possible, however, that the Windego may still be lurking around the Roseau area to this day if the story told by a young man named Brad is any indication. I met him in early 1995 through some mutual acquaintances, and in casual conversation, my interest in the sasquatch came up. Brad said he knew very well of the Windego legend around Roseau, that the Windego is still seen there today and that he and some friends had actually seen it themselves from inside a car on January 18, 1992, and captured it on videotape. This is potentially very important, of course, but as of this writing, I have not seen the tape in question and am not sure of Brad's whereabouts. Perhaps the future will reopen this case. However, it should be noted that Brad was sure the Windego was a spiritual being and not a physical animal.

In another modern Indian account, there are similar circumstances told by a young man named Neil, who I met just briefly in 1995. I'm sure little attention will be paid to this one since he was quite intoxicated when he told of it, but his emotional state tended to lend believability to the story. He was a member of the Ojibwa tribe from the White Earth Reservation (not far from where my own childhood sighting occurred) and was having a bit of a depressive episode, lamenting about the prejudices he and his people suffered in the white man's world. He then started describing his strong spiritual beliefs and experiences, telling of various mystical events he had witnessed at Indian gatherings on the reservation. In the midst of all this was the description of how he had once watched a sasquatch about eight feet tall for a period of one minute not long before. He did not dwell on it long, going on to other matters of importance to his present state of mind. It's hard to tell about stories like that, but the White Earth area is certainly good country for hiding the creatures.

(I should point out that I don't for one second mean to imply that most of these Indian stories are the result of too much alcohol. This particular person just happened to have a problem with it.)

The Indian story I have the most experience with comes from the southeast part of the state and is a truly amazing one. On July 23, 1988, the Red Wing *Republican Eagle* printed the following article:

GIANT FOOTPRINT SIGNALS A TIME TO SEEK STRENGTH

PRARIE ISLAND - The discovery of what appears to be an 18-inch long, humanlike footprint on Prarie Island Indian Reservation is more than a curiosity or topic of conversation among the tight-knit community.

To Indians living here who follow traditional beliefs, it is a signal to find renewed spiritual strength at a time of difficulty.

Wayne Running Wolf was sitting in his living room on the reservation at about 9:30 p.m. Thursday when his dogs began barking frantically. He said he noticed something out of the corner of his eye through a window as he got up to see what the commotion was about.

"I saw a shadow or a shape, but I don't know exactly what I saw," Running Wolf said Friday.

"Whether it was a shadow or a shape, I don't know," he added. "I'd be a liar if I claimed either one. I thought someone was messing with my car."

"Our dog in the house, he was barking at the same time," added Dwight Wells, a neighbor.

What Running Wolf did discover, and has no doubts about, were two huge footprints crossing his driveway and heading toward a nearby wooded area. One print became obscured in the soft sand, but the clearer one definitely appears humanlike, with five distinct toes on the end.

What outsiders might easily dismiss as a hoax is seen by several spiritual leaders here as a sign that Cee-ha-tonka, referred to simply as "the big man," has paid a call.

"We have our old legends about 'the big man,'" Running Wolf said. "If it exists, it exists. You accept it." Common misunderstanding of Indian culture and sense of spirituality may cause some to scoff, "but I know what I'm looking at," Running Wolf said, carefully covering the print under a wheelbarrow.

"That big man, he's been around for centuries," Wells added. Both men referred questions about the meaning of the big man to spiritual leaders.

The big man appears "mostly near where there are Indian communities that are struggling or having problems," said Amos Owen, spiritual head of the community. "That's a message for us. But the people are afraid of it."

The Prarie Island community is in grief this week over the untimely, accidental death Thursday of 27-year-old Clayton Wells, Dwight's brother.

A sign is always left behind after the appearance: a footprint, a musky scent, a tuft of hair, or broken tree limbs too big for a normal-sized human to smash, he said.

"In our way of beliefs, they make appearances at troubled times," said Ralph Gray Wolf, an Alaskan spiritual leader visiting Prarie Island. He helps those troubled communities "to get more in tune with Mother Earth" and gain spiritual energy and inner strength. With the renewal comes the ability to face the difficulty.

Before appearing, the big man sends "signs or messages that there is a need

to change, a need to cleanse," Gray Wolf said. "Right afterward, is when he makes his appearances."

"The legend has a way of teaching you. It disciplines you in certain ways," said Ray Owen, Amos' son. "It's to make you become more aware of other things."

The sign of the big man is preceded by a sense of foreboding among the tribe, he said, adding he could sense that before this week.

"I was up in Minneapolis, and I just had to get back down here," he said. "I felt that pressure, that tension."

The trio said the big man has appeared in many Indian communities: Standing Rock, N.D., Pine Ridge, S.D., even Prairie Island five years ago, to name a few.

Legends of a "bigfoot" or "Sasquatch" among Indian tribes of the Pacific Northwest, along with claims of footprints, photos, and other purported evidence, have been sensationalized in the same class as the Loch Ness Monster and UFOs.

But for some Prarie Island residents, it is a time of looking quietly inward and seeking spiritual guidance.

Scientists have tried to debunk the evidence of the big man's existence, Gray Wolf pointed out, "but they've never been able to disprove it."

In July of 1989, I took a brief tour of southeast Minnesota and stopped at Prairie Island (which is actually neither a prairie nor an island) to look into this. I managed to locate Wayne Running Wolf, and he expressed how he was very reluctant to talk about the incident and didn't even know how it had gotten into the paper. That someone had phoned it in anonymously, but he confirmed everything it said. He said the Big Man had much to do with his peoples' religion, and so they didn't like to talk about it to strangers who wouldn't understand. I asked if he knew of anyone else who had seen the creature, and he said, "Probably everybody on the island at one time or another."

He took me to the home of Amos Owen, the spiritual leader of this Sioux tribe. It was a mystical type of place, with a teepee in the yard next to the house to remind visitors of ancient days. But as it turned out, the man was preparing to go on a trip and didn't wish to see anyone at that time.

Before I left, Running Wolf added one point to the story. The 18-inch tracks, he said, had eagle feathers in them, ancient symbols of strength to Indian people.

I resolved to return someday soon for a more extended stay in the area to search for this so-called Big Man. That time came in May of 1990. I pitched a tent near the edge of the Vermillion River and explored the local woods, and what I found was what I considered a perfect (although confined) habitat for a sasquatch. High, rocky bluffs, overgrown with foliage, rise from the river's edge, and below the level of the bank, there is a long stretch of wet, spongy ground on which you can look back and see your footprints rising back up. If a creature was to come down from the woods to these swampy flats to catch the slow-moving dogfish (large, carp-like fish) that swim in the muddy shallows, its tracks would never be found. I saw several kinds of animals, but unfortunately no sasquatch.

I did, however, pay another visit to the Indians, which turned out to be the high point of the trip. There was a pow-wow going on in honor of Memorial Day where I found Dwight Wells, who had been mentioned in the 1988 newspaper article. However, he did not wish to discuss the incident, so I went to the home of Amos Owen to see if I could have better luck this time in getting to see the spiritual leader, but when I asked to see him, I learned that he had fallen ill and wasn't in any condition to talk to anyone.

Out in the yard, a number of people were gathered around a fire preparing for an evening sweat lodge ceremony. (The sweat lodge is basically a small dome-shaped sauna in which men share a ritual of spiritual bonding.) Among them was Wayne Running Wolf, who I spoke with again. I discovered that he is one of the tribal priests and also that by blood, he is an Iroquois from the east coast area and was accepted by the Sioux after moving to Minnesota. He is an interesting man, but even more so was the man he introduced me to, Ray Owen, acting spiritual leader while his father was ill. While sitting by the fire with him, I heard all he had to say about the Big Man.

I did not record the conversation, for it was a rather nervous moment as the Indians decided whether or not they wanted to accept me in their presence, but later I wrote down as much of what was said as I could recall. Here, in no certain order, are several near-quotes from both Running Wolf and Ray Owen:

Ray (upon seeing a picture from the famous 1967 Roger Patterson sasquatch film from California): "That doesn't look like the ones I see. They're more human.

But then, they can look one way to one person and another way to another person, however they want to look to get their message across. Whenever they appear, there's a reason, a message. We had a guy here back when that story in the paper happened, boyfriend of one of the girls here, saying he didn't believe all our old superstitious nonsense and that the Big Man didn't exist. Then he was out in the woods just back over here (gestured), and the thing appeared right in front of him, stared right into his eyes. Then it turned to walk away and just vanished into the air. That's the way they can do it. They exist in another dimension from us, but they can appear in this one whenever they have a reason to. See, it's like there are many levels, many dimensions. When our time in this one is finished, we move on to the next, but the Big Man can go-between. The Big Man comes from God. He's our big brother, kind of looks out for us. Two years ago, we were going downhill, really self-destructive. We needed a sign to put us back on track, and that's why the Big Man appeared. If you really want to see one, you should kill everybody around here! (A joke, naturally)

"Every tribe, no matter where you go, knows the Big Man. Where I felt him the strongest was by Hoopa in California. See, sometimes you can feel him, you can sense when he's around. I was driving along when my car died, and when I got out to look at it, I could feel him real strong. There wasn't even anything wrong with the car, it started right up again. There was some reason why I was supposed to sense him at that time. They got a big sign there, 'Entry to Bigfoot Country.' I really laughed when I saw that.

"(More on the Patterson film:) There had to be a picture taken, some proof that he was real, so he let himself be photographed to show that the Indians were being straight about him. Now, he can have his pissed-off side too, and he can be violent. The Indians could have used the Big Man to defeat the white man in all their wars long ago, but they didn't. They should have, but it wasn't meant to be. Everything has a reason. We were meant to be absorbed by the white man, and the Big Man saw to it that there would be peace. So he let himself be photographed to show that the Indian didn't lie.

"(Upon hearing of my own 1976 sighting:) You were very blessed to see one.

Now, you tell me you saw one, and that's enough. Indians talk straight, we don't lie, and I'll take you at your word. (Shook my hand.) There had to be a reason why you saw it. You say only you saw it and no one else in the car? That was because he appeared only to you and was invisible to everybody else. One could walk through this yard right now, and if he didn't want to be seen, nobody would see him. Or maybe only one person would see him. You keep looking, you'll see another one. Maybe it'll only be for a second. He'll just go in and out (gestured), just like that, and then he'll be gone. You have to be in a wild, lonely place. Maybe up north, up in the boundary waters. They're not around here right now, probably up north."

Wayne: "It's like I said before, if it exists, it exists. You just accept it. Like the one I seen that time."

Myself: "Is that the only one you've seen?"

Wayne: "No."

Myself: "How many others?"

Wayne: "Well, I can't tell you that. There's stuff we're not allowed to talk about. I mean, I've walked with the Big Man. There's children here today that've played with him. Just about everybody around here has seen him at one time or another, but we don't talk about it to white men. Now, we mix with them pretty good.

We go into town to buy food, they come out here to look around, but you'll notice that there's a few white people here today, but mostly we're all Indians. We keep a lot of stuff to ourselves. We speak English most of the time, but that's because there's a mix of different tribes and languages here, like me being an Iroquois, and we have to understand each other."

Myself: "If the Big Man only appears when he wants to, why do you think there are so many white people who see them, like when they're driving along at night and happen to see one standing along the road?"

Wayne: "That's just it. They just happen to see one. They get lucky. Now, if that was an Indian driving along, maybe he'd stop and talk with him.

"(Upon hearing where I was exploring:) You were up in those hills?"

Myself: "Well, no, just along the bottom. It's pretty hard to get up there."

Wayne: "Yeah, well, I'd keep you off's those hills. That's sacred ground, we have ceremonies up there. There's things up there that no white man would ever understand. You keep looking around long enough in places like that and you might see something that you wish to God you had never, ever seen."

Additionally, when asked if the Big Man could be killed if someone got a shot at him, Ray said, "You could shoot him with a bazooka. You could drop a nuke on him. You can't kill a spirit."

When I left the area that evening, I felt like I was in the twilight zone. I stopped in Bloomington on the way home, and it took a long discussion with investigators Mark Hall and Tim Olson to bring me back down to Earth.

Sadly, a week or so after returning home, I learned that Amos Owen had died. It wouldn't surprise me to learn that Cee-ha-tonka had shown up to pay his respects.

In other regions, I was told that the Indians in the Bemidji area know full well of the sasquatch there but almost never discuss it with outsiders, and in Clearwater County, Ed Trimble heard an old Indian legend about a mysterious spiritual being that leaves behind footprints on the winter ice to mark its passage through the world of men. (As you will see in later chapters, this became quite an ironic tale for Mr. Trimble.) These would both be Chippewa stories.

But after some years in this business, I can now say that the Prairie Island story is actually a fairly typical portrayal of how tradition-minded Native Americans view the sasquatch, not just in Minnesota but all over North America. Occasionally one finds more of an element of fear involved. There are always those communities where Indians have become "modernized" to the point where all or most of their knowledge of ancient legends has been forgotten. Still, the usual relationship between the Indians and Sasquatch is viewed as one of great respect.

For the record, I believe the sasquatch is an earthly, physical animal and not some ghostly being. This is not to be argumentative with the Indians. They are good people who are comfortable with their beliefs and will not be dissuaded by any outsiders' opinions. And who is to say that they do not see and experience all that they claim? There are many strange and wonderful things in this world that go beyond human understanding. If forced to come to a conclusion on the matter, though, I would say I think it is very significant that many tribes believe that virtually all animals are the embodiments of spirits, not just the sasquatch. Legends of the great bear spirit or the spirit of the deer, however, or of the talking ravens that frequently appear at the scenes of major events in Indian history, fail to capture as much attention in the sensationalistic media as does a "big hairy monster."

Still, we should listen to our Indian friends when they share their colorful and exciting culture with us. There may be more for us to learn than we might think about our place in nature. Whatever the truth, I have the utmost respect for these people and have considered myself very privileged to be allowed into at least a small corner of their world.

The home of Wayne Running Wolf at Prarie Island, where the Big Man appeared.

2

SUPERIOR - THE DEEP WOODS

The Superior National Forest in northeast Minnesota is a truly vast wilderness. At roughly 175 by 90 miles, it is undoubtedly the most extensive such area in the state, and in its remoteness, it rivals the great forests of the Pacific Northwest.

In the western part of this region are iron ranges such as the Mesabi and Vermilion, centers of industry where iron ore is mined and around which several towns are situated. As one travels east, however, one sees fewer and fewer signs of civilization until, in the heart of the forest, it seems as if time has reversed itself to a point before the coming of the white man. Finally, there is the rocky shore of Lake Superior, the largest of the Great Lakes, where human habitation is again apparent along a coastline that looks for all the world like that of an ocean, complete with lighthouses. In following the coast southwest a short distance, one comes to Duluth, the "San Francisco of the North," one of the most important shipping centers in mid-America.

Not surprisingly, this stunningly beautiful area is popular with tourists, especially the northern section. Here Voyageurs National Park marks the entrance to the Boundary Waters Canoe Area, a rugged region of connected lakes, inlets, and small islands that one could explore for weeks without seeing it all. Cross over to the northern side of these waters, and you are in Canada, the southwestern part of Ontario that contains Quetico Provincial Park and even more thick, unspoiled forest land.

It may sound like a broad statement, but if the sasquatch does not exist in the Superior National Forest, then it does not exist at all. With the lack of people and the almost prehistoric remoteness of the forest's interior, it is a perfect habitat for the creatures. One thing I've noticed is that the Boundary Waters Canoe Area, in many respects, resembles the remote, island-dotted coast of British Columbia, where convincing evidence has been found that sasquatches may be very adept swimmers.

It may seem somewhat odd, then, that there are not a lot more sighting reports from this area than there are, but this is probably due to a lack of potential witnesses rather than a lack of creatures to be seen. Many people camp in the forest each year, but they do not begin to cover all of the potential hiding places for the hairy giants.

I believe it was in the Superior region that one of the first reported sightings by white men in Minnesota took place, second only to the story of the Windego at Roseau a decade earlier (see previous chapter). Ivan T. Sanderson, the famous biologist who specialized in studying mysterious phenomena, wrote of the incident in his book "Things" (1967), giving the location as the "northern tip of the state." This could be any of several different places, actually, but it seems to refer to the pointed shape of this particular part of Minnesota, which is in fact known as the Arrowhead Region.

The year was 1911. Two men were hunting near a town (name not given) when they came across some strange tracks. They followed them through the woods and eventually caught sight of a "human giant which had long arms and short, light hair, covering most of its body." After they lost sight of the creature, one man remained while the other hurried to town and rounded up a posse to hunt it. Although the group then searched for some time over a considerable distance, they found nothing but more of the odd footprints, which were not described in any detail.

That's a fairly mundane story compared to the one told by Nancy Mostad, who now works for Llewellyn Publications in St. Paul, one of the country's foremost publishers of New Age and paranormal material, including *Fate* magazine. Some years ago, I was trying to do some business with Llewellyn, and as an addition to one of her letters, Ms. Mostad wrote:

"As a child, I saw what I called a big white gorilla who would come out and stand on the treeline as I played in the meadow. I felt it was a very protective presence and never felt any fear. This was in northern Minnesota."

In a follow-up, she wrote:

"That big white hairy friend of mine came out of the woods every time I played in the meadow. He always stayed right at the tree line and just watched me.

I have a hunch about him, but it would seem silly, so I just keep it to myself.

He stayed around for about six years."

A brief report like that can be quite a teaser, but the full details came out when Tim Olson did a telephone interview with Nancy in January of 1992.

This is really quite a unique story.

TIM OLSON: Nancy, my name is Tim Olson, and I am a good friend of Mike Quast. I understand that you were in contact with him a couple of years ago, and you had written to him saying that you had seen a Bigfoot-type animal in Minnesota, which you called a white gorilla.

NANCY MOSTAD: Yeah, that's when I was a kid.

TIM: Could you go into more depth for me?

NANCY: It was something that I noticed in our meadow when I would go out to play. This started when I was about six, and I would see this big white-like gorilla, and it was really big and really noticeable, and he would stand right on the treeline. It's like he wouldn't cross over into the field. He would just stand there and watch me.

TIM: He would stay behind the trees out of sight?

NANCY: No. He would stand right on the edge of the treeline. He was always visible to me, but I could see where other people might see him blending in, so he could step back and not be seen.

TIM: Is this during the wintertime?

NANCY: During the summer. In the winter, it was too dark for me to go out there and play because it was a ways from the house. This went on from the time I was six until I was 13. I had my cousin Jennifer over, and we were out there, and we were sitting and talking as 13-year-old girls will talk, and I said to her, "Jennifer, do you see that white gorilla standing against the trees over there?" Well, she couldn't see him, and she thought I was just crazy, and I thought, well gee, maybe I am, and after that, I never saw him again.

TIM: Maybe you were just hallucinating?

NANCY: Yeah, but I'd seen him for seven years, and I was a pretty normal farm kid. We had farm land which bordered the Superior National Forest, so there was a lot of forest. We had wolves in our forty, and I kinda' felt like he sort of protected me because the wolves would come out in the meadow and play too, but I never had a problem with it when I was growing up.

TIM: Did it ever make any sounds or noises or gestures to you or anything of that nature?

NANCY: It just watched me. It just watched me constantly.

TIM: What color eyes did it have?

NANCY: They were sort of just like dark orbs. I mean, they weren't like eyes. They were just like dark spaces in the face.

TIM: Where was this exactly?

NANCY: This was about ten miles north of Chisolm, Minnesota.

TIM: The years were what?

NANCY: I would say about 1959 through about 1965.

TIM: Why do you think it didn't show up after 1965?

NANCY: I think because I blocked myself from seeing it, you know, I just didn't look for it 'cause I didn't want anybody to think I was kooky or anything.

TIM: Crazy, huh?

NANCY: Well, it was funny because I kept trying to point him out, and I was so shocked that she couldn't see him, and Jennifer was like, "No, there is nothing there."

NANCY: No, it wasn't hard for me to see.

TIM: How tall or big was this?

NANCY: It was big. I would say it was between eight and ten feet tall. It was very broad-shouldered and very wooly, very long fur.

TIM: Your cousin didn't see it?

NANCY: No. I tried to talk to my mother about it, but she said, "Don't talk about such silly things." So, I didn't talk to anybody about it, and I just always felt... At first, I was afraid when I first started seeing him, and I'd run home.

But then, after a while, I realized, well, he never did anything, he never came at me, he just sort of watched me. Then it got to be where I felt sort of protected like I didn't have to be afraid of wild animals and things when he was around. I was just a little girl and far enough away from the house that I would have been vulnerable to larger animals such as wolves or bears. Not that they would have harmed me, but you know what I mean.

TIM: Did it ever make any movements, or did it just stand there all the time?

NANCY: Oh, it moved. I would see him move its arms and he would kind of turn this way and that. He was always watching.

TIM: Would you say he was observing you?

NANCY: I felt observed, but I also felt that there was, um... well, this is going to sound really silly, but there was a mental communication between us that didn't need to be verbal. It wasn't in the form of words so much as it was in the form of, um... a sort of a comfort. Almost like having a playmate kind of thing. I felt that he was very much alone.

TIM: Lonely?

NANCY: I don't know about lonely, but very solitary. There were no others like him there... I think he was alone for whatever reason. I guess my feeling is that those kinds of beings cross over different planes of existence, and he may have been alone while he was in my plane of existence at that time. But the way he was able to move in and out and be there whenever I was there and then gone, and other people couldn't see him, I just have to believe that it was something that, um... I don't know, he had some particular reason that he was around me. A protector, an observer, or whatever.

TIM: Are you the only person that actually saw this thing?

NANCY: Yeah. You're 13 years old, and you're having a conversation with your friend, and you just happen to mention this thing stand there about, you know, a good ways away but still very visible. She was like, "Oh really." And she thought I was trying to scare her, and I said no, no, that kind of thing.

TIM: But she did look to where you pointed to?

NANCY: Yes, she looked, and I pointed it out, and I pointed out the trees that he was standing between and that kind of thing.

TIM: Do you think that this could have been a one-on-one experience?

NANCY: I think so. I think it was. I think there was a reason that he was there. I've never figured it out, but when I think back to my childhood, that was one of the very special things about it. My mom was ill a lot of the time, and my dad was always gone working. Basically, I was alone all the time. When I would go into the field to play, then he would come there, then it was like I wasn't alone.

TIM: So it's very much like that imaginary playmate that kids fantasize having around.

NANCY: Yeah, in a sense, but I could see him, and communication was sort of heart to heart without being verbal. It had long, thick legs, a thick trunk of a body.

TIM: But always by trees or in them?

NANCY: Not always in the same spot. Always in the treeline though, but he would not cross over into the field. He was always so that he could just step back into the foliage. Listening to such a story, it's hard to believe it's not an Indian telling it. It has such a spiritual nature to it, I'm sure the residents of Prairie Island would raise an eyebrow or two at this tale. Several years after these strange events, there was an incident of a much more conventional nature in the same area. I learned of it when the witness, initials W.F., wrote to me after seeing an article on me and my investigations in the November-December 1991 issue of *Minnesota Calls* magazine. His account was short and to the point:

"We always thought our experience had to be a bear since we had not heard of any sasquatch 'sightings' in Minnesota. You are the expert, tell us what you think."

"Time: Late July- 7-9 p.m. 1989."

"Place: St. Louis County Road 5 to Side Lake, MN north of Hibbing/Chisolm."

"50-75 yards in front of our car, this animal crossed the road running upright, moving faster than we believed a bear could run. He seemed too large to be the type of bear that would be around this part of the country. That was all we saw of him. Your thoughts?"

Bears do not run on their hind legs, of course, so it is quite possible that this road-running creature was a sasquatch, but more details would be needed to be sure.

Moving east a short distance to the edge of the Vermilion iron range, another strange beast appeared in early July of 1972. The story was told in *The Tower News*, July 21, 1972.

WHITE "CREATURE" SIGHTED NEAR TOWER

Perhaps shyness is one of the characteristics of the creature, which was sighted on two occasions recently in the vicinity of the Charles Trucano home in rural Tower. Following the excitement and publicity when it was seen twice within a week, the creature appears to have retreated into the woods- or wherever "creatures" go.

The stark white creature was first seen about three weeks ago when Debbie Trucano, 13, and her boyfriend were playing badminton near the house. It was just at dusk when Debbie glimpsed "IT" in the woods. She described "IT" as being four and a half feet tall, about three feet wide, and pure white in color.

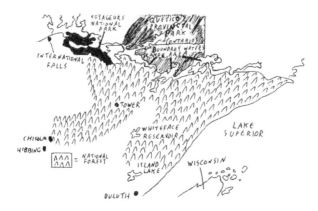

| Map showing locations of reports in the Superior area.

It headed back into the woods, and the noise of the breaking brush could be easily heard as it made its retreat.

Less than a week later, again, just at dusk, the creature was seen in a sand pit on the Trucano property. Billy Harve of Tower, David Galaski of Virginia, and Michael Trucano, 21, and Bob Trucano, 17, saw "IT" emerge from the woods. They hurried into the car and drove home to get Mr. Trucano. Returning to the sand pit to search for "IT," they found a distinct trail trampled through the woods but could see no sign of the creature. This is the last sighting which has been reported, but the family is uneasily awaiting further developments.

The Trucano farm is located about a mile and a quarter west of Tower on Highway 169.

This odd white dwarf did not reappear, but half a year later, one of its relatives may have turned up about 50 miles to the south. On January 26, 1973, a boy named Bob McGregor, age 11, saw another white creature at his home on Island Lake north of Duluth. This one was considerably larger, standing 8 feet tall. It walked through the family's front yard and then, appearing curious, went through a nearby unfinished house under construction before departing the scene.

There seems to be a trend in the Superior region toward white-haired creatures. Why this should be, I have no idea, but there are also darker-colored examples.

Ray Crowe, an investigator in Portland, Oregon, publishes a newsletter called *The Track Record*. In his January 1992 issue, he featured the following account from someone known by only a first name.

"In 1978... Roxanne went to visit her daughter and 22-year-old brother near Lake Superior in rural Minnesota. Leaving her brother behind, they went to town on a late errand. All of a sudden, he said there was this 'god awful smell', and the dogs started barking and making a commotion. He thought a skunk had gotten in the chicken house and took the gun to investigate. Using a powerful 'spotlight' type of flashlight, he was met by Bigfoot. He had ripped a hole in the chicken wire fence and was standing with a chicken in his hand. He said the thing had a 'peaceful' look on its face... the thing started a deep-toned chatter from deep in its throat. The witness stood paralyzed, dropped the rifle... and blew a hole in the side of the chicken house. After the rifle went off, the thing let out a scream.

The dogs ran under the porch and were cowering on top of each other... When the rest returned home, they found him in a dazed condition, crying... and repeating 'nobody's gonna believe me.' He finally told them what he had seen, describing the thing as dark with a human face, with no snout. It had fairly long hair, and the hands were human.

"Next day, dad found the chicken wire enclosure ripped with tufts of hair hanging from it. There were 18-20" long very clear footprints in the yard that ran across a muddy meadow and led into the woods that back up to Lake Superior where there are acres of swamps."

Here we have an example of a commonly reported trait of the sasquatch, their foul odor. Many witnesses have described it as being quite overpowering, but others report no smell at all. What might cause it has been a mystery to investigators.

I wish the originator of this story had been a little more specific as to the location since the shore of Lake Superior in Minnesota covers an awful lot of territory. Virtually all of it, however, is likely sasquatch country.

There was a report in a 1970 book called *Strange Abominable Snowmen* by Warren Smith about a couple, Mr. & Mrs. J.H. Allen of

Dallas, Texas, having seen a sasquatch rummaging through their campsite in the "Superior-Quantico National Forests," date unspecified.

I listed this report in one of my earlier books on Minnesota, but after further study, it now seems that it actually took place in Ontario. Mrs. Allen mentions crossing the border at Ottawa Island. "Quantico" is probably a mistaken reference to Quantico Provincial Park. Still, this would have been in the heart of the Boundary Waters Canoe Area.

I have a reference to another report from the BWCA, passed on to me by Tim Olson. He was talking to a man about some incidents in South Dakota (see chapter 22) when he said he knew another man from Ely, Minnesota, who had seen a sasquatch at Fall Lake up in the Boundary Waters in 1980. Unfortunately, I lack any further details.

Finally, mention should be made here of the alleged experience of Frank D. Hansen at the Whiteface Reservoir, 40 miles north of Duluth, in late 1963. It is just one small part of the incredibly complex "Minnesota Iceman" case and will be dealt with fully in its own section.

I have no doubt that there are other sightings to be uncovered in this pristine wilderness, sightings that no one has ever ventured to report. Perhaps in time, they will be revealed, but for now, they and their subject lie hidden in the depths of the great boreal forest.

3

SWAMP CREATURES

Harvey Cole was charged by an angry female black bear protecting its cub in 1989. He stood his ground, waving his arms and yelling like a madman, and the bear turned away before it reached him. Moments later, he broke a tree branch over his leg to use as a weapon in case the bear returned, not realizing that it would have been much too thick for him to snap had there not been adrenalin rushing through his body.

This is only one of many exciting stories that Harvey can tell after 30 years as a technician for the Minnesota Department of Natural Resources. His best ones, however, have to do with a very different kind of animal.

Harvey lives and works in a wild area in the middle of northern Minnesota, bordering Canada, most of it lying in Koochiching County. This region is much the same as any other wilderness area, but it has the added distinction of containing "Big Bog Country," or what is probably the biggest swamp in the entire state.

If you try to research the history of the sasquatch in this region via old news clippings, this is what you will find (from the July 13, 1979 edition of the International Falls *Daily Journal*):

SASQUATCH HUNTER LOOKS FOR THE BEAST IN KOOCHICHING COUNTY

Richard Johnson knows it is a mammal. He figures it is a little bigger than a human, but not by much, and its arms are a little longer than normal. It probably lives underground, walks on its hind feet, travels mostly by night, and stays in one vicinity for only a week.

And Johnson believes it has a mind bordering the intelligence of humans, a sixth sense "that almost has the ability to sense your presence."

"It" is Bigfoot, or Sasquatch, or whatever.

Johnson not only believes it exists, but he says there's a good chance Sasquatch roams the woods of Koochiching County.

The 33-year-old St. Paul man has pinpointed two quadrangular - one in Koochiching County just south of Margie and another near the Bear River in Itasca County. Sasquatch also may be found in the general areas of Craigsville and Crane Lake, he says.

He began writing letters this spring to various rangers in the area in an effort to acquire topographic maps of specific sites. He also wanted to let game wardens know of his intentions in case permission was needed to conduct his search. Copies of Johnson's letters finally arrived on the desk of Jim Schneeweis, area wildlife manager with the Minnesota Department of Natural Resources (DNR).

Johnson claims he sighted a Sasquatch in November 1978 near Margie.

"It was not as heavily built as I thought it would be," he said via telephone from his St. Paul apartment Thursday. "It had a reddish tinge to its fur. I saw it enter the swamp."

Johnson says he's quite familiar with wildlife and knows the animal was not a bear, which is about the only animal in Minnesota that could be compared to a Sasquatch. He tracked that one for a while but then lost it.

He spotted footprints just this past March too, which he says were narrower than he thought they would be.

He plans to return sometime yet this summer or early fall before hunting season begins. Johnson, a carpenter, is out of work now due to an injury he received while on the job. He has a wife and child. As soon as his finances allow, Johnson says he will begin another search.

"You don't know if you're going to see anything or not," Johnson says. "But it's a beautiful country, and you get to see a lot of wildlife. This time I will be equipped with a good camera."

Johnson has no certain method when conducting his searches. Since the forest is so dense, he noted a compass is a necessity "You put a camp up and look and listen. Then you move in and look and listen again."

His interest in Sasquatch began several years ago when his brother worked for Boise Cascade Corp. in Walla Walla, Wash. At that time, the area was in a frenzy over reported Sasquatch sightings. But Johnson claims that only was a publicity gimmick and estimates that 75 percent of those sightings were fictitious.

That type of publicity led to the closing of the national office for Sasquatch research, he says. Sasquatch is an endangered species under the Endangered Species Act of 1973.

(Note: That paragraph is false, either through a misquote of Johnson or his own mistake. There was no actual "national office." This probably refers to Peter Byrne's Bigfoot Information Center in Oregon, which closed in 1979. And the Endangered Species Act would not recognize an animal that is considered mythical by most scientists.)

"A great percentage of people believe this is some sort of gimmick," he says.

But Johnson believes it's real and that possibly half a dozen roam the woods of northern Minnesota. He's been following the saga of the Sasquatch for about 12 years but did not take a serious interest until he spotted one in 1978.

Johnson is not alone in his theory that some strange animal lurks in the forests.

Harvey Cole, a district technician with the DNR office at

Northome, was one of the men contacted by Johnson. He confirmed that unusual sightings have been reported over the years.

One instance, he recalled, occurred in the winter of about 1965 when footprints trailed off the road and across a swamp. It was in the area south of Margie, exactly where Johnson suspects Sasquatch might exist. "The snow was 3 feet deep," Cole said Thursday. "No man would ever go there and come back alive."

A neighbor of Cole's, Chipper Lowe of Northome, was working in the woods by Marcell during a recent summer when Lowe and his friend spotted what they thought was a bear, Cole said. They evidently went to the lakeshore to see what damage the animal had done, but it had disappeared. Later that night, Cole said, something shook the trailer where Lowe and his friend were sleeping. They never discovered what caused the disturbance, Cole said. (See chapter five.)

"That's the exact area where Johnson said the Sasquatch was," Cole said.

Several other people across the country also have claimed Sasquatch sightings and produced photographs, but nothing ever was proven, Johnson explained.

Other than his wife, Johnson says probably no one else knows of his desire to find the Sasquatch. He wants to keep it that way.

"I really play this down. That's about it. If I happen to find it, there's a law protecting them. If I could find one and trap it, I would probably turn it over to the zoological society for scientific purposes. That's the only interest I have."

And Johnson is not about to be swayed by all the gimmickry surrounding the search for Sasquatch. But he believes it exists and says, with help, he hopes to find it during his lifetime.

"I'm a realistic person," he says. "I believe only in facts."

Eleven days later, the same paper ran a tongue-in-cheek article by columnist Harry Davey entitled "Sasquatch? There are 100s of them."

in his "Rainy River Reflections" column, basically laughing off the whole business and paying special attention to the creatures' "reddish tinge:"

The July 13 edition of the *Daily Journal* had a front-page story about a St. Paul man who believes a strange humanoid, known as Bigfoot, Sasquatch, or whatever, exists in Koochiching County. The gentleman plans to come to the county late this summer or early fall to continue his quest for Sasquatch.

We admire the inquisitive mind and the spirit of adventure of this gentleman, but we can save him a lot of time and money. The "mystery" is easily explained, to wit:

> "There are, without a doubt, Bigfeet, Sasquatches, Sasquatchi, or whatever, in Kooch County. Yea, there are hundreds of 'em."

They are so common that most permanent residents, and most newcomers, know all about 'em. They are so numerous, they are taken for granted. They arouse no unusual curiosity, they are completely harmless, and they appear only temporarily. They are similar in appearance to the fictional Dr. Jekyll and Mr. Hyde. But they are not similar in character, as there is no evil in them.

These Bigfeet, Sasquatchi, or whatever, roam hither and yon throughout the broad reaches of Kooch County every autumn during dates set by the government of this great state. During those days, the Sasquatchi are given their freedom to change character, change appearance, and travel the forestland unimpeded, free from inquiry and illegal search and seizure, providing they obey the laws of the land pertaining to the season.

It is true that a stranger in the land, sighting a Sasquatch scurrying through the woods or scampering across a public highway or logging trail, would be filled with fear, along with curiosity.

Its appearance is not especially attractive, except for patches of bright red easily visible to even the most frightened pair of eyes. It is usually scraggly in appearance. If it's rather late in the Sasquatch season, the face is covered with a heavy growth of matted hair that gives it an apelike appearance. The eyes, sometimes bloodshot and only half open from lack of sleep, give it a sinister appearance that utterly belies its friendly nature.

It will speak in an intelligible tongue if spoken to, but the stricken stranger is in no mood to stop for a chat. The stranger is driven by a strong urge to get to the nearest town and the nearest tavern to quiet his quaking nerves.

If the St. Paul gentleman wants to come to the Falls and continue his study of Sasquatch, I would like to refer him to my friend Elmer Henrickson. Elmer has hosted scores of Bigfeet over the years at his logging camp in the Pine Island State Forest. He is probably the country's foremost authority on the Sasquatch, its habits, foibles, favorite food and beverages, and its mode of life during the Sasquatch season.

Elmer will confirm the fact that Sasquatch is more human than humanoid. At the end of the season, it will return to its normal life as a human. It is only during the season that it takes leave of its real character, its job, its profession, its wife, its family- and sometimes, take leave of its senses.

Elmer even has an excellent photograph of a Sasquatch. It is a picture of a Sasquatch arising from its bed in the early dawn. It is clad in something that closely resembles long underwear, and it wears an expression of complete exhaustion.

The picture is entitled "Daylight in the Swamp." The picture would win no prize at an art show, but it would answer a lot of questions for the St. Paul gentleman.

Though trying to be humorous, Davey seems to have actually thought the sasquatch phenomenon could be written off as sightings of wayward deer hunters.

I have tried to locate Richard Johnson a few times. A St. Paul address was found for him, but I learned that someone had looked for him there and come up empty. I suspect that he may not have even been using his real name since he seemed to want to downplay his investigation.

Be that as it may, sometime after adding those two news clippings to my collection, I learned that, for one thing, the paper had given both the date and location incorrectly for the tracks seen by Harvey Cole, and also that they had barely scratched the surface of what has turned out to be a rich treasure trove of interesting reports.

With a buildup like that, I almost hate now to have to lead off with a story that is sure to cause an emotional controversy and make my fellow investigator wonder what's wrong with me if I fully support it. Nevertheless, it is just such a tale that lies at the beginning of the sasquatch's history in this area. It was told to Ed Trimble by a neighbor in Clearwater County who had been describing his own sighting down there (see chapter 14). The original source is not known.

The story goes that in about 1910, some loggers in the International Falls area are supposed to have captured a sasquatch. They kept it in a cage of poles and fed it for a week, but it screamed and fought terribly and finally escaped before an expert that had been notified could arrive to examine it.

Now brace yourselves, sasquatch enthusiasts. The loggers called the creature Jocko.

Well, we in the field all know that "Jocko" or "Jacko" was the name of the creature in the very famous story from Yale, British Columbia, in an 1884 telling of a young sasquatch captured by a railroad crew. I'm fairly certain that there is just some confusion here among the people who told and retold this story over the years and that it is a mix-up with the 1884 story. How it got placed in Minnesota 26 years later is anyone's guess.

I suppose, though, that there may be a slight chance that this is a version of something that really did happen at said place and time and that the loggers could have named their creature after the more famous one after reading old newspaper accounts since Canadian papers in 1884 did carry the Jacko story.

Mr. Trimble has tried to find out more but to no avail. This looks like one report in which the truth will never be known, and I take no responsibility for the blasted thing.

Less controversial but still undocumented is another story Ed heard about from around 40 years ago, which would put it in the early to mid-1950s, involving a seven-year-old boy who is said to have seen a sasquatch at a fairly close range west of International Falls. It was crossing a road, and both the creature and the frightened boy froze upon seeing each other. The creature stood and stared for a moment, then continued on. Another anecdote to add to the collection, but unfortunately not very useful today.

I would much rather share with you a remarkable account of the close-up sighting of a large adult sasquatch by an experienced wildlife observer near the town of Waskish, in the heart of the bog country.

While at a county fair Ed Trimble met a man who said he knew someone who had seen one of the creatures, and Ed wasted no time in contacting him. He wrote the introduction to the transcript of the taped interview that follows:

"The printed page cannot convey the excitement, surprise, and wonder the way 35-year-old Lee Cluff's expressive voice does as he vividly recalls his close-up sighting. We- Ed and Nova Trimble- met Lee and Sharon at their pleasantly located north Bemidji home (on Friday, August 22, 1991). It was a nice evening, so we sat on the porch. The only distractions were nice ones... Sharon bringing us lemonade and a couple of deer venturing near enough to cause Sugar, the Cluffs' big, friendly dog, to bark.

"Except for a brief phone call when I first located Lee and asked for an interview, we hadn't met. So we just visited and got acquainted, took a look at John Green's books, and read parts of Mike Quast's "Sasquatch in Minnesota." For us, it was very rewarding to see the relief Lee was experiencing as he began to see that several others had had sightings in this state and that a cluster of such

is shown on page 6 of Quast's book within short miles and the same general timeframe of his!"

LEE CLUFF: I was thinking about the time when I had my sighting... I know it

was in the year of '76, and it was in the early, early, early summer... We were

what they call yearding out wood from the winter wood supply in the woods, you know, that was back off the main road that we had large stockpiles of spruce, 200 cords of spruce and we were moving that into town and then down toward Kelliher and on up the highway and up to International Falls. And I was just trying to picture in my mind— I know when I seen it I always wanted to remember this, and how was I ever gonna remember this thing, what could I connect it with? And there was a holiday there, and I told myself I'd never forget that holiday. Now you ask me 15 years later, and I can't remember that holiday (laughs). But it was right prior to planting season. So it was probably Memorial Day or Easter, 'cause it could've dried up early that year.

I've never told this story before— only to my wife and my three brothers, and a forestry man, but like I say, back in the year '76, which is quite some time now already, we were yarding out wood out in the bog up in Waskish, my father and I. We were in the truck. We were traveling west on County Road 40, which is straight east of Waskish. It runs east and west there for about six or seven miles. We were at the very eastern end of that road, and we had just put on a full load of spruce, and we were headed west— this was about five o'clock at night, and the sun was setting pretty low like it would be in the spring. I remember it was so low because the sun was coming right in the windshield at us.

My father was driving the truck, and I was riding in the right seat, and we started coming back toward Waskish on this ditch road, we were going along about 30 miles an hour, and we'd probably gotten two miles down the road, three miles down the road...

and I seen a creature step out of the woods, across the bottom of the ditch— and the ditch bottom was probably three to four feet wide, right at the bottom— stepped across the ditch, swing his arms out, and it was looking back at where he had stepped out of the woods from. He looked back over his shoulder.

He was tall, black, and with thick hair. And the thing that stood out in my mind was the legs, the long gait he had, and his long arms. The closer we got to this thing— I seen this point-blank, right in front of me— the closer we got up to this thing, the animal turned its head and looked directly at the truck that I and my father were in, 'cause he heard us then— he was looking back— and he looked right at us, and he looked me right in the face. He was looking right at the front end of our truck. Just momentarily-- took three more steps and walked right back into the woods where it had came from. And ah, the detail with which I seen this animal— the only reason I'm having this conversation, I guess, is because, ah... it's something I don't tell anybody— it's something I seen. My father didn't see it. He was looking in his rear view mirror. We had a large, tall load on and it was shifting on us, and he was watching it. I hollered to my dad, I said, "Dad, what is that?" And when Dad turned around, the sun glare was in his eyes, worse than it was mine on the windshield, for whatever reason I don't know, but just as the thing went into the woods, he got his eyes focused, and he didn't see it. He said he just— he thought he seen something just leave into the woods line, but then that was all he seen. But I got the full-blown picture of this animal. I would say it was between six-five and seven-foot-tall, three to four hundred pounds, and it turned and it walked back into the woods, at a fast gait.

And— other parts of the thing that I seen that I can, you know, recollect now after 15 years later that stand out in my mind is the look on that creature's face when it looked at me and didn't realize I was there, and I was looking at it first. And then it turned its eyes, turned its head, and went back into the woods and disappeared. I remember vividly too, we got down the road— after I said to my dad, I said, "What is that?"— actually my words were "What the hell is that?" - my dad, you know, he just swung right over, and ah— in fact, the first motion he had was to hit the brakes, 'cause he thought there was a problem, and I told him exactly what I'd seen, and I was really excited. I was really pumped up at this time. And when he slowed the truck down— started slowing down, slowing down and I was telling Dad, I said, "Dad, did you see what I seen? Did you see that thing?" (Laughs.) And my dad said, "No, I was looking in the mirror." And I know Dad was looking in the mirror 'cause he was watching the left side of that load...

And ah, for three days after that — and my wife can confirm this

— I was kind of a different person, 'cause I'd seen something I had never read or heard or imagined even seeing, you know? I didn't know what it was. So the next morning, the morning after I had my sighting, I drove down to Bemidji, and my sole purpose that day was to report it to the DNR officials at their offices in Bemidji, which is right adjacent to the university down here. And they, ah— I told them what I'd seen— they didn't disbelieve me, and they didn't say that they really believed me... They knew that what I was telling was a fact. I told them the facts, what I had seen, and I left. And the first time I heard anything about this since was approximately two weeks ago... when these people here, they'd heard that I'd sighted one and they wanted to know my story. Now there's a lot of details I probably left out, but basically, that's what I seen.

ED TRIMBLE: So it had real long arms.

LEE: Real long arms.

ED: And it swung them.

LEE: That's the thing that caught my eye, mostly... I have long arms. I'm six foot five myself, and that thing had arms a lot longer than I have. (Laughs.)

ED: Did they reach down to its knees or below?

LEE: It didn't reach below its knees, no, but it reached to its knees...

Like I say, the animal was six foot five or seven-foot tall and probably weighed between 300 and 400 pounds. You know, according to a man's size and dimension and weight. And it was slightly stooped, like I said all covered with hair... pointy little head, a tuft or something pointed on its head, and its eyes were hazel—

almost could see its eyes like a hazel dark black— and a real dark face, and it

had distinct eye contact. That's the most thing that amazed me. That thing looked right— see, he was looking at the front of the biggest thing that was coming at

him, that he didn't know until he looked at it, and he looked right at me right in

my eyeballs, 'cause I was sitting in the seat, and I was looking right over the hood of the truck. And he looked me right square in the eye. That's the thing that got me. And I think that's the thing that made me tell myself that, yes, I did see

Bigfoot, or sasquatch, whatever that is. When you get eye contact like that, you know (laughs)— I mean, you really have eye contact! With something that, no, it's not a deer, no it's not a bear, no it's not an elk or a moose or a — I mean — it's a Bigfoot. There's no way around it.

But the thing that impressed me too is when it stepped across the ditch bottom, and I know the ditch bottom is four to five feet across. At least — you know, it was well over four. And he stepped across that thing in one step, and his next step he was headed up on the in slope of the road. And all the time he was doing this, he was looking back where he was coming from, at that tractor out in that field... turned around and looked me right square in the eyeballs. Turned right back around and made three steps, and he was gone. And he covered about 30 feet... 25 to 30 feet, and he was gone, and I remember it 'cause I can still remember seeing that brush move. I seen it that good.

ED: Would you say he was real muscular?

LEE: Muscular like a gorilla, no. No. No, he was thinner than a gorilla— much taller, of course— but yet weighing, you know— I estimate six to seven feet tall but still weighing three to four hundred pounds. You know, he definitely had heft to him... Heavy, strong shoulders and chest and back muscles... He had a big heavy waist and pretty good-sized legs. They were long. But no, nothing like a gorilla at all. As far as being really, you know, like a wrestler. He wasn't, ah... not that much. It definitely had buttocks. They didn't protrude like something with, you know, big buttocks, but they were pronounced enough that I could see them... I didn't see any privates.

ED (later in the interview): Do you think that someone should shoot something like that or not?

LEE: No way. I know we're all curious people... but, you know, me shooting something like that is definitely out of the question. There's no way. Just 'cause you don't understand it and don't know what to do doesn't mean you shoot it. I'm a pilot myself. When I was in Alaska, I flew a lot of planes up there, and I've seen a lot of wildlife. Moose, grizzly bear, I've seen a lot of things -- I've never seen anything like this. I've seen wolves kill moose right from the air... I seen a lot of things when I was in Alaska but never seen anything like that day in '76 up there at Waskish. Never. And I don't think I ever will again.

Lee later elaborated on his description of the creature by saying that its color was not exactly black, but it was very dark. His recollections are extremely vivid and detailed even after so many years, a testament to the impact that encounters with these animals can have on people.

We come now to the aforementioned Harvey Cole. After I first met Tim Olson, I learned that in 1986 he had done a taped interview with Harvey at his DNR office in Northome. Here is a transcript of that interview, which supplies the true date and locations for Harvey's track report:

HARVEY COLE: My name is Harvey Cole. I work for the Department of Natural Resources in northern Minnesota in the lower part of Koochiching County, and I've been at this position for going on 25 years now. A lot of our district involves the Big Bog country to the north, which, looking at a state map, lies north of Red Lake, clear to the Canadian border. And the first account of running into anything that was as strange as could be Bigfoot was probably back in 1978 or so. I was cruising timber with two other fellows on a small island out in the bog, and we ran across— this was in the winter time when the snow was deep, probably 30 inches of snow. We were on snowshoes when we came across what looked like a man had walked in a north-south line. Huge prints, in the bottom of the print they were probably 12 to 16 inches long and seven to eight inches wide. Snow had drifted into them, and these tracks were probably four foot apart, so whatever it was had a long stride, and I never seen anything like it before. So I followed the tracks up for a ways till I came to some hair found in a black spruce tree that some animal had rubbed up against, and I had assumed the track had to be either a bear or a moose, and upon examining the hair sample, I was convinced it wasn't a moose. I didn't take the sample, which I wish now I would've 'cause it probably would have been fascinating. Now at the time, I wasn't thinking about Bigfoot or anything, so I never gave it a second thought, but I was certain that it wasn't a bear track because the pace and distance of the tracks, it was a much too rangy an animal to have been a bear. So I kind of just forgot about it as one of those things that, you know, you see, and you don't know what it might have been. A while later, I was talking with a cruiser from Koochiching County, and I mentioned this track that I had seen in the snow, and he related that he had seen the same track about the same time because he was working in an area about three miles north of where I was and whatever this creature was had gone to the country and he had hit his track also. And I guess that's about all I can tell you about that one.

Then it was about '79 or '78, maybe, there was a contractor building a big transmission line that runs across from northern Minnesota from Manitoba down toward Duluth. This line is a power-poled constructed of an aluminum girder-type construction, and we had sites where they would put these things together, and then they would ferry them on their helicopter into the bog, and they would be set on their base. There would be a crew there that would bolt them down. The fellow that flew the helicopter had spotted a beast that would cross this powerline, whatever it was, once in a while, but he just figured it had to be a bear or a moose or something and never paid any attention to it, although it was probably pretty hard for him to while he was carrying one of these power poles that are about maybe 70 or 80 feet tall dangling below a helicopter so you have to pay attention to your business, so he couldn't follow the animal.

In the spring, as the snow went off, the beaver trappers frequent the bog— that's got a network of old ditches in it— and I know that a beaver trapper that went in his canoe from Highway 72. He got about two miles east of the highway when he intersected with the power-line, and in a clearing of the right-of-way of the other powerline, there had been a pile of brush pushed up, and when he approached this pile of brush, this Bigfoot stood up. It scared him pretty bad, and I guess he said the thing ran down the powerline like a quarter of a mile, and it ran on its hind legs all the way. He was apparently pretty darn close to the thing because he said when it stood up, it had a... his face wasn't completely hair-covered, you could see some facial features. He said his butt wasn't haired like the rest of his body, but he said the whole animal was pretty hair-covered. He said it had a large (male organ), that this was a noticeable thing right away when the creature stood up and looked around when the creature heard the banging of the canoe on a little beaver dam that wasn't very far from there. He watched it run away, and that's as far as he went. The creature scared him enough, and he had seen enough, so he turned around, and he left.

TIM OLSON: Did he say if it made any noise?

HARVEY: No, there was no mention that it made any noise at all. It just stood up, I guess and turned, and he seen his facial features, and the creature turned and ran. It ran away from him, which would be down this powerline, and then went into this timber.

TIM: Did he mention anything about any kind of odor?

HARVEY: Not that I... I don't think he stuck around to notice or look for anything because he paddled back the two miles back to the road, and he drove to a station in Waskish and wanted the game warden to report it to, but there was no one around.

Map of the Koochiching County area where sasquatch reports have occurred.

I guess the guys he told it to, they kind of laughed at him or something, anyway he drove back down the road another 17 miles to Kelliher to the forestry station there, and he reported it, what he had seen. They kind of questioned him about it and got more details on it, and after work that evening Vince Buck, the district forester at the station, he and two or three fellows that went with him and took plaster of Paris and they were gonna go up and take footprints and cast the footprints. So they go up there, and they had to hike in there, and it's two miles through the bog, which took them longer than they had anticipated because of the heavy going. When they got to the site, they found impressions of footprints. They said you could follow and find them down the powerline, but the bog is composed of mosses and little bushes, and it's all fibrous material, and to find a footprint that you can get detail out of, you can't. You can find impressions, but you can't find an actual footprint with toes or great detail of a footprint. So they picked a good print, as good a print as they could find, and they made their plaster of Paris and put it in the track. It was getting really late, and they had to get out of there, so they put colored ribbons around some bushes there, and they left. Their intentions were to come in the next day and pick this print, which due to other obligations and stuff, they never did. It went on, and they just plain forgot about it to go back and pick up the print.

Time went on about two years, and we were gonna have a county fair here, and we were talking about things to put in our displays, and I mentioned to the supervisor about this footprint which had never been picked. So he says, "Well, go get it." So I drove up there, and I walked in the two miles to this particular area where this footprint was supposed to be, and I had inquired of Vince Buck of how to find it, and he gave me the details of where he made the print, and I found it. The interesting thing that I found along the way was this powerline had been in operation, I suppose a couple of years by then, but there's a path under that powerline from pole to pole, and it's a couple feet wide and is well dented down, the moss and stuff, like a foot deep and as time goes on it's going to get deeper. But there's been something that is traveled under that powerline with padded feet.

TIM: Regularly?

HARVEY: Regularly, yes. At the time I was there... well, I'd say to make a path like that, it would've had to be traveled maybe a couple times a month or so. The impression on the trail is really good, and you can just walk right along the trail. I don't know why it's there. The powerline makes a noise— the line hums, and also, you can hear the static electricity just a'cracklin' in those lines. People tell me if you stop under that line at night, you'll actually see the cracklin' noises actually light up up there, and apparently, whatever made this path under here is attracted to the powerlines for some reason. I followed this path a long ways under the powerline that day when I went to lift this foot. When I got to the print, I don't know; I suspect it's from the acid in the bog water or something. I found the print; it was intact and everything, but I could not lift it out of there. Every time I would get a hold where I could pick it, it would crumble. The plaster of Paris was just plain rotten. So I couldn't lift it intact, so I left it, and I assume it's still there. I just couldn't do anything with it, I just left it. I looked around for something similar, but it's— you know, you gotta find something like that, and in the bog, it just gradually erases itself too because it's a sponge, and it gradually disappears.

TIM: When you saw the track, how definite did it look as far as a footprint?

HARVEY: It looked to me like it could've been a footprint all right because [of] the shape of the plaster and everything, it just looked like it probably was a big footprint and I don't doubt the fellow that put it there put the plaster in there, and they picked the best print they could find. I've seen bear trails that they use in the summertime; they'll approach a waterhole and put their foot in the same track each time. This wasn't that type of trail; it looked like it maybe could've been made by a family group of some kind, each guy's stride was a little different, so he stepped in a different place. It was a well-padded trail.

TIM: How far back did you sink when you walked on it in relationship to the other tracks?

HARVEY: It didn't seem like I sank at all compared to what were in those trails.

TIM: So whatever, it was heavy.

HARVEY: Yeah. Whatever uses that padded trail is much heavier than I am.

TIM: How much do you weigh?

HARVEY: I weigh 170 pounds. I assume if I traveled on an area like that, you'd make a trail all right, but I don't think a man would end up making a path like that.

TIM: How many pounds would you guess?

HARVEY: Well, I'd say whatever is using the trail is probably 300 pounds. Considering the size of his feet, he was considerably heavier than a man. You'd have to be pretty heavy to make an impression in that kind of ground like that.

TIM: What year was it when you went back to pull out the track?

HARVEY: I'd say probably '80 or '81, right in there somewhere.

TIM: Has anyone ever been back there since?

HARVEY: Not that I know.

TIM: So tracks still might be being made, but no one knows about?

HARVEY: Well, since that time, there could be. But since that time, I heard no more about any sightings of any kind. There was a period in there of about four or five years when there was more than one sighting made in the International Falls area, which is only 30 miles or so the way the crow flies from this area or 35 miles, so it's not that far away. So there was a period of about five years in there when there were different observations that I had seen in the bog and then this little one the beaver trapper had seen, and then this Mr. Johnson that had seen one on the highway south of Margie (mistake- it was not on a highway) and a couple sightings in the Littlefork area, International Falls area. They were all within probably a time frame of about five years there. Since that time, I haven't heard anything on it. My theory is that if there is one living in the bog along that power-line, maybe it was zapped by the powerline too, 'cause something attracted them to follow under the line, and maybe they climbed them too, I don't know. It's something that they were inquisitive about, or they disliked about it or something, but they were attracted to follow under that powerline.

TIM: Do you know if anyone has been back there since?

HARVEY: I assume the power company has their maintenance crew back there, but I think most of that is done by helicopter. They fly the line every once in a while to see if anything needs to be done.

TIM: This trapper guy that goes back for beaver, doesn't he ever go back there anymore?

HARVEY: I never ever heard no more of him. Whether he seen too much or what, I don't know, but I never heard of him coming back. But there's other guys that travel the bog at different times of the year. You don't penetrate the bog unless you have a purpose to go out there, for it's just that tough a'going. It's some place that it just plain hard going for anybody to want to penetrate it on foot. It's tough, tough walking. You walk three or four miles out there in the bog in a day, and I'll guarantee you won't want to walk any farther. We just don't go out there unless we have management things we gotta do, and that's usually done in the winter time where the ground is froze. So you got people that are active around the edges of the bog or on some road that crisscrosses in there so there could be something out there and could spend as many lifetimes out there and nobody would observe them 'cause nobody has a reason to go out in the bog. That's why they can remain unseen forever.

I can easily visualize the events Harvey speaks of because I have seen and experienced the area in question myself. In October of 1992, having already become familiar with the land surrounding the bog and having stood on Highway 72 watching the famous powerline stretch out across it, I vowed to finally penetrate this swampy morass myself. I quickly found out that Harvey wasn't kidding about how hard it was just to walk through it. It is one of the least friendly places I've ever encountered in my travels. The walking is even worse than trudging through deep snow, totally exhausting. Stop to rest, and in some spots, you start to sink. It is not really open water and not solid ground, but a strange, spongy combination of the two, dotted with small evergreens. Large animals (and humans) leave well-defined, long-lasting trails as they smash their way through, but all I saw was a deer and beaver sign. However, I didn't begin to cover enough area for a really thorough search. One thing is obvious: it would indeed take something substantial to make a trail through the bog, such as Harvey Cole described.

I have heard that deep in the bog, there are old houses built decades ago, partially sunken in the ground but otherwise well preserved in the state they were left by the people forced to abandon them. The land refused to accept human habitation.

If Harvey's theory about the creatures being electrocuted by the powerline is correct, the bodies could easily have lain there decomposing, right out in the open, virtually forever without anyone coming along to find them. The bog is nature's way of saying, "Humans are not welcome here."

There was a rather strange track find during the same time period as the other events to the northeast of the bog. It was detailed in Ted Steiner and David Warner's *Minnesota Bigfoot News*, issue 29, drawn from the *Minnesota Times*:

"On a muddy farm road on James Erickson's property, 12-inch tracks were found. Their greatest width was *Ah* inches, with a stride of 3 1/2 to four feet. Six toes, a large ball, and a very high arch. Made after a heavy rain. No sign of vehicle or other prints around. This line of prints started and finished in the center of a muddy road."

While looking through "File 3300- Bigfoot," a loosely assembled collection of letters, tabloid clippings, and other assorted material at the Northome DNR station, I came across a more detailed account of this incident in a clipping from the familiar International Falls *Daily Journal*, September 14, 1979...

HE WON'T SAY WHAT MADE THAT BIG FOOTPRINT

Kerry Meyers wasn't going to make a big deal out of it. The big footprint he made a plaster cast of a week ago while looking for a deer hunting spot near Littlefork, that is. That's right, a big footprint. Six toes on each 13-inch foot.

And he'll be the first to tell you he really doesn't care who or what made the prints on a mud trail north of the Harold Erickson farm northeast of Little- fork.

"Everybody thinks I'm trying to pull something," he said, "but I just found them. I didn't fake 'em, and if someone did, they went to a lot of work."

Meyers, who lives in the Falls, was out searching for a bow hunting spot in the evening with his father-in-law John Seitz, Bemidji, when he discovered the footprints. It was just after a rain, and the ground was soft, he explained. "I was driving along in the jeep and looked over at some wolf tracks and saw this footprint. It was barefoot, and I thought to myself, who'd be running barefoot way out here. So I stopped and looked."

It was getting dark, so he left but returned the next day and made a plaster cast of one of the prints. He found five prints in all that showed the six toes. Three from a right foot and two from a left foot.

"I've counted them over and over again, and there's six of 'em for sure.

"And one thing's for sure. It wasn't anybody that was in my gym class.

"I can't figure it out. If someone faked them, they did a darn good job and didn't leave any other prints around there. The prints go right through a bunch of mud holes, and I can't figure out why anybody that was running wouldn't have tried to go around them. He went right through every dang one of those things."

Meyers says he doesn't think he's going to hunt around there after all. At least not all the way to sunset.

Now the obvious question: Six toes?

There are many reports in the sasquatch field involving footprints with less than five toes, but when there are more, we are faced with a real oddity. I can only recall two other such cases, and they were in Colorado and Wisconsin. We can only assume that some kind of mutation must be involved.

As for the tracks seeming to materialize and vanish in the middle of the road, well, I have seen rabbit tracks do the same thing. There are those who will try and make something supernatural or para-normal out of this but be assured it can and does happen through perfectly natural means.

The next sighting involved Stanley Sunderland of Clearwater County, a friend, and neighbor of Ed Trimble's.

It was a yearly custom for Stanley and his sons, David and Rodney, to go fishing up in Canada. On May 3, 1980, they were returning from the trip on Highway 11 near International Falls, not far from the Canadian border. The two sons were evidently not paying very much attention to the surrounding scenery; thus, they missed the amazing sight their father, 51 years old at the time, suddenly beheld.

I conducted the following taped interview with him in 1991:

STANLEY SUNDERLAND: We left from fishing up in Canada in the forenoon, and we was traveling through this area about 2:00 in the afternoon. It was right west of International Falls six, seven miles. I was looking at the right-hand side, I was sitting on the right-hand side, and the boys were driving; one boy was driving and one in the center. And then I seen this here thing going across the field, and it looked, ah— like a gorilla. But it looked to me like, you know, I thought it was running — I just thought it was a gorilla at the time. I just — it never dawned on my mind it could be anything but that. And ah, it was long hair on its head, you know, streaming out behind it as it was running across that field. And ah—

I don't know what more I can tell you about it. It looked like a man, but it looked like a gorilla too, you know. To me, it did, you know. But it was brown and hairy, you know. That's what I seen, anyway.

MYSELF: About what size was it?

STANLEY: Probably about— 250, 300 pounds, somewhere in there. And probably about six foot tall, it looked like... It was out there probably 300 feet about, you know. And he looked clean; it was a good view of him. It was just that short distance, not a very big field, you know, that he run across. But I don't know what I can tell you otherwise... but it was something strange. (Laughs.) Whether it was reality or not, I'll tell you is beyond me. I don't know what else it could be.

Stanley apparently didn't know that gorillas do not run on two legs as this creature did. The rest of the description is also quite unlike the great ape. He noted that the hair streaming out behind its head and neck was as much as 18 inches long, much longer than that on the rest of the body. He didn't get a look at its face, but the body was muscular, with arms about to the knees, rather short legs, a short neck, and a slight peak to the top of the head. Everything happened too fast to observe much more detail. He alerted his sons immediately, and they turned the vehicle around for a look, but the creature had disappeared into the woods beside the field.

In a remarkable coincidence, Stanley's son David had had a sighting of his own, completely unrelated, 10 or 12 years earlier near their home in Clearwater County (see chapter 14). It's a small world sometimes, isn't it?

More recently, Ed Trimble also heard a vague report about a timber operation in the Big Falls area, run by a man with initials A.K., where there may have been some type of sasquatch activity in about 1990. Unfortunately, nothing more is known about it at this time.

At about the same time, two women are rumored to have seen a sasquatch crossing the road between the communities of Gemmel and Mizpah. This was told to Ed and me by the wife of track-finder Troy Parson (see his story in chapter 17).

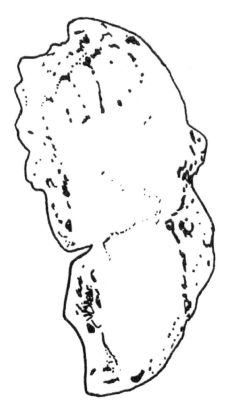

Drawing of the plaster cast of the six-toed footprint found by Kerry Meyers near Littlefork, taken from a photo in International Falls Daily Journal, Sept. 14, 1979.

Stanley Sunderland drew this sketch of the creature he saw near International Falls on May 3, 1980.

The most dramatic event of 1990, though, was undoubtedly the experience of a Mr. Lammers and his 12-year-old son in the Miz- pah area. This was told to me by Marion Senn, a researcher from Otter Tail County whose main field of interest is UFOs and extraterrestrials. However, she is also interested in the sasquatch, especially since she had a creature sighting of her own in 1994 (see chapter five).

Mr. Lammers and his son were deer hunting, which would make it November, and had just come back to their pickup truck toward dusk. They sat in the vehicle waiting for two companions who were still out in the woods. Suddenly they were surprised by the appearance of a gorilla-like creature about six feet tall and very heavy and muscular, with dark brown hair, which grabbed the back of the pickup and began violently shaking it. It made strange, angry grunting sounds.

After a few moments of this, the creature crossed the road along which the truck was parked and picked up a rock about 30" wide, demonstrating great strength. From a distance of 15 feet, it then threw the rock into the truck box, denting the metal six inches deep. Finally, it ran off, leaping almost effortlessly over a brush pile in its path.

It was the boy's first-time deer hunting, and he hasn't been back since.

Incidents of this kind, though rare, are usually interpreted as territorial displays, with the creature saying, "This is my woods, get out of here." (A remarkably similar incident occurred north of Bemidji in 1993 - see chapter five.)

I do not believe it can be said that the sasquatch is an entirely peaceful and benign animal that is never a danger to man, as many writers are fond of implying, but the same is true of most animals. Even deer have attacked people on rare occasions. I tend to consider the sasquatch about as potentially dangerous as the average bear, which usually runs from a man but should be treated with great caution.

Finally, we come to the end of this exciting saga back with our old friend Harvey Cole. As you will recall, he had been thinking that the sasquatches were no longer in the area since shortly after the coming of the powerline. However, in the spring of 1991, he was on the

Gemmel Ridge, checking the condition of some newly purchased woodland, when he again came across the familiar big tracks. They were in melting snow, but although the toe impressions had blurred together, most of the prints were still clearly defined. They measured 17 inches long by nine inches wide and did not look like shoe or boot prints.

I've always been glad we have Harvey around. It's a rare thing for a government forestry official to both believe in and openly talk about the sasquatch.

In the middle of the town of Northome, there is a large wooden statue of a bear and a sign welcoming visitors to "Big Bear Country." The local garbage dump is often filled with the tracks of foraging bears, and it's obvious that they are very plentiful in the area.

As many of the locals will tell you, though, bears are not the only large hairy creatures that roam their woods and swamps.

4

THE HAIRY MAN OF VERGAS TRAILS

This is the story of how I got started in this business.

Those who follow the various publications relating to the study of Bigfoot/sasquatch may have seen brief mention of the Vergas Trails "Hairy Man," written by myself. The details of this story make it one of the more exciting ones in the annals of sasquatch lore anywhere and certainly one of the most intriguing such cases in Minnesota.

The location is in the western part of the state. The town of Vergas lies in Otter Tail County. Ten miles to the north, in Becker County, is Detroit Lakes. Situated midway between these two towns, there is a large section of about 30 square miles made up partially of farmland but mostly of lakes and some of the thickest forest for miles around.

A large portion of the forest has been unofficially named "Vergas Trails" due to the dirt roads that wind their way through it. These trails are a popular recreation site among local young people, although they are not labeled as such on any map. In fact, much of the woods in the area are privately owned by various farmers and other local people. Still, favorite activities there include mud running in four-wheel-drive trucks and nocturnal parties that leave scattered empty beer cans in their wake. These mostly harmless activities have gone on undisturbed for many years, with the forest remaining relatively unchanged.

There are three main roads and several smaller ones branching out from them that make' up Vergas Trails, most marked with signs reading "Minimum Maintenance Road- Travel at Your Own Risk." Indeed, it is easy for cars to get stuck there when spring and summer rains turn the dirt to mud, and in the winter, the only vehicle capable of getting through is a snowmobile, another popular form of local recreation. In recent years, ATV cycles have also become common in the area. I can attest to the driving conditions in Vergas Trails, as I once crashed into a tree there along an icy road.

Several lakes, both large and small, lie in and around the area. In the eastern section are three rather unimaginatively named ones, Lakes Five, Six, and Seven, the largest being about two miles long. Smaller lakes of about 1/2-square mile, Lake Ida and Cooks lake lie in the west, and in the southwest corner are two large ones connected to each other, Leek and Trowbridge, which will figure prominently in the story that follows.

There is a single farm within Vergas Trails, but two ancient windmills and a few scattered ruins mark the spots where others once stood decades ago. There is also a summer camp right in the center, Camp Cherith, where kids enjoy recreation in the warmer months. Summer cabins dot the shores of the larger lakes, and there are many rural dwellings just outside the trails at the edge of the forest. Cattle are sometimes pastured in a few different locations. A final sign of civilization is a power line that runs through the woods. Its high steel towers look strangely out of place amidst the surrounding trees.

Wild dogs can sometimes be found in the area, most belonging to farmers but occasionally getting together to live a feral life in the woods until the comforts of home beckon them back. They have caused quite an annoyance for wildlife officials by chasing and killing deer, and once on the opposite side of Detroit Lakes from

Vergas Trails, a pack of such dogs attacked and injured a woman and child who were walking along a highway at night after their car had stalled.

Nature at its worst, one might say. And as you will see, it's hard to tell just what else might live in those woods.

Vergas Trails has a sinister side, a spooky side. It is a place where young people tell stories to frighten each other on dark nights, stories that are supposed to be true. There is always exaggeration in such tales, of course, but many legends are based on fact.

It is rumored, for instance, that a bizarre religious cult once used the area for mysterious nocturnal gatherings, performing strange rituals. In fact, I used to know a girl who became involved with this group. They were active in the late 1980s but were last reported to have moved to Texas.

Then there is the legend of the Hairy Man. It is still told today, though not as frequently as in the 1970s. Seldom are the storytellers serious anymore, and none of the present generations have probably seen the being they speak of. To them, he is a piece of local folklore and nothing more.

The most common version of the tale goes like this: Years ago, sometime in the 50s or 60s, a crazy old man murdered some teenagers for some unknown reason and then fled into the woods north of Vergas to hide from the law. (If this crime ever actually occurred, there is no record of it, a fact which about sums up the validity of this particular tale.) He became a hermit, living off the land, and as time went on, he became wild and grew hair all over his body. He may still be out there, the kids say, watching our every move.

(Recently, while hiking in Vergas Trails, I discovered an old abandoned hunting cabin deep in the woods that made me remember this wild tale. It was in ruins, but painted on its side was a large round target and the words "Keep Walking.")

Although I grew up on a farm north of Detroit Lakes, I never heard of the Hairy Man until the late 1980s. By that time, the greatest excitement over him had long since died down, but in 1987 I had begun to get actively involved in sasquatch research. I was talking to my somewhat older brother-in-law one day when he mentioned the Hairy Man and related to me the above story as he had heard it in his teenage years. What immediately came to mind was a sasquatch, so I pressed him for more details. When was all this supposed to have happened?

Who told you about it? Did they actually see this Hairy Man?

He could not remember everything. It had been a long time, after all. He had never believed a word of it in the first place. Still, he thought he remembered a friend from Detroit Lakes saying that he had seen something strange one evening at about sunset while snowmobiling in Vergas Trails, something dark and humanoid in shape but larger than a man, walking along a ridge atop a valley where the powerline cuts through the woods. He could not recall the year, but probably sometime in the early 1970s.

It certainly sounded intriguing. But it couldn't be, I thought.

A sasquatch- living for an extended period of time so near to my home without me ever once hearing about it in all these years? My own childhood sighting wasn't all that far away either (although in the other direction), but I had always considered that a very isolated incident.

Could the Hairy Man have been a sasquatch that found its way to Vergas Trails and stayed for a few years, remaining fairly unknown except by rumor because no one who saw it ever reported it to authorities? I doubted it at the time, suspecting that the whole story was just a tall tale, but I had to find out for sure, so off I went on my first real sasquatch investigation.

I contacted my brother-in-law's friend and visited him at his home in Detroit Lakes. No, he said, he was not the snowmobiler in question (and if that sighting did take place, the witness has yet to be identified) and had never seen the Hairy Man himself, but he certainly remembered the stories, and he happened to know someone who definitely claimed he had seen the creature. He gave me the man's name: Ken Zitzow.

Ken, or "Ziggy", as his friends call him, is a mechanic living at the edge of the woods beside Lake Seven north of Vergas. I talked with him on January 26, 1989, in his workshop, ringed by the forest that makes up the edge of Vergas Trails, and this is the story he enthusiastically told me:

On a clear October night in 1969, Ken, then 16, was out with his older brother and the brother's girlfriend driving around with no particular place to go. He was driving while the other two sat in the back seat, traveling through a wooded section near Vergas Trails (or "The Klondike", as they called it).

Suddenly, without warning, something leaped into the road from a ditch (a 20-foot jump, he said, as if it was "spring-loaded"). Ken couldn't believe his eyes as the thing stood with its arms raised up as if to stop the car, but it jumped aside at the last second, and he passed by.

"Holy (so-and-so)!" he shouted. "Did you see that? A hairy man! It was a hairy man!" The others hadn't seen it, but when Ken turned the car around for another look, there it still was. All seven or eight feet of it. A cross between a man and a gorilla, weighing about 300 pounds and covered all over with black hair.

"Hit it!" his brother yelled in the pandemonium. Whether this meant hit the gas or hit the creature is not clear, but in any case, Ken sped forward. As he did, the beast struck out with both of its hands, and the trio heard a loud thud against the rear of the car.

Later they found a large dent in the trunk lid, so bad that it had to be replaced.

With that, the first sighting was history, but Ken was excited now and, with some friends, began looking for the creature again. They spotted it a number of times, running through fields in the moonlight, during the fall. Then winter came, and it seemed to disappear. They wondered if it might be hibernating.

This suspicion seemed to be confirmed in the spring of 1970 when the group found an old, abandoned wooden shack just across a road from Leek and Trowbridge Lakes, not far from where the first sighting had occurred. A trail of trampled grass led to it, and a huge open space had been dug out beneath the shack. Could it be a den? Inside the hole, there was an old beaten-up spring mattress, plus the strong, foul smell of a wild animal in the air.

Ken was nervous and wanted to leave quickly, but the group was apparently not very happy about having such a beast in their neighborhood, and eventually, they decided to take action.

This old windmill and a few other ruins mark the spot where a farmstead once stood in Vergas Trails.

A man stands in a ditch at the approximate location where the Hairy Man leaped out at the Zitzow brothers' car in October, 1969.

This hole is probably the remains of what may have been the Hairy Man's den in the winter of 1969-70. A wooden shack stood on the spot then.

They surrounded the shack with straw bales and set it on fire, burning it to the ground. After that, they never saw the Hairy Man, as they called it, again. (I have found the spot where this supposed den was. It has deteriorated now to a large waterhole and a few pieces of wood that may have once been planks. And personally, I doubt that sasquatches actually hibernate, but they may seek shelter from harsh weather in such dens.)

In further describing the creature, Ken says of its face simply that "it had two eyes, a nose, and mouth, you know, everything where it was supposed to be." It also had a thick beard that covered its neck. Overall, he said it had a manlike body and an apelike head.

He doesn't know what became of the Hairy Man, nor does he really care since he would not like to see it again. He once told me, "If you go after that thing, you better have plenty of firepower."

After hearing this story, I got very busy trying to find out if anyone else had seen the creature. I contacted one man who, Zitzow said, may have seen it, initials D.S., but he himself had a different story. He said that he had, in fact, once dressed up as the Hairy Man "to scare some girls." I am certain, though, that this was well after the creature was already locally known.

Then a letter to the editor of the Detroit Lakes newspaper produced an unexpected response. I received a letter from Paul Lindstrom, a young teen living in Marina, California, who spent his summers with relatives near Vergas. They had sent him a copy of my letter, as he happened to be very much into "Bigfoot" studies. He said he knew of two other incidents in the Vergas Trails area from as recently as 1978.

One case involved a group of teens who had seen the creature and gone to get a shotgun, but when they returned, they could find no trace of it.

The other story was of a farmer who had had so much trouble with the Hairy Man raiding his cabbage patch and killing his dogs that he had moved away.

Paul was short on specifics, but I was thankful for the information just the same.

Meanwhile, I started searching the area as often as I could. Months went on, and I didn't find anything. At one point, I came across a deer that had been killed by wild dogs, and occasionally I would run into a couple of the skittish canines, but that was about the extent of the excitement. I was fast becoming convinced that there was no longer a sasquatch to be found there.

Then, on August 31, 1989, I made a discovery. At the bottom of the valley through which part of the powerline runs, there were some strange tracks in the dirt. It had been raining; thus the first track I saw, out in the open, was not very clear. It measured 16 inches long, 7 1/2 inches wide at the toe end and 6 1/2 at the heel end, and was not very deep. The toes had all blurred together, but the foot seemed to have a slight arch. Thirty-seven inches beyond were two round impressions two inches deep that could have been heel marks. I decided to make a cast of the print, and on the way to my car to get the plaster, I stumbled across a second print. It was slightly under cover and thus more distinct, 16 inches long, ten inches across the toes, 4 1/2 inches wide at the heel.

Three-toed Vergas Trails footprint, found August 31, 1989.

There were three toes, very clear. It was about 135 feet from the other print.

Since three-toed sasquatch tracks, as opposed to more normal five-toed ones, have caused such controversy, I had always hoped never to find any, but unfortunately, I did, and I could not ignore it. I thought one animal was probably responsible for both prints, the width difference being due to rain damage or other variables.

The clear print couldn't be easily cast due to the slope of the ground (the foot had molded perfectly over a slight bump, ruling out a rigid "fake foot" that a hoaxer would use), but I did cast the other one. While waiting for it to dry, I heard something moving in the woods, breaking branches about 200 feet away. Probably a deer, I admit, but who knows? I believe this was about where the alleged snowmobiler sighting was supposed to have happened.

That find gave me new enthusiasm, as did the similarities I found later with the events up in Koochiching County (see chapter three) where sasquatches seemed to be attracted to a powerline. The line in Vergas Trails is of the same type. Interestingly enough, DNR technician Harvey Cole's son, living way up in Koochiching, had heard of Vergas Trails even though many local people don't even know about it.

According to Marion Senn, UFO researcher from Otter Tail County, there was another incident in 1989 that involved more than just footprints. She heard about it second-hand, and as I did not meet Marion until 1994, I had no idea that such things were still going on while I was poking around in Vergas Trails.

In the spring, possibly late April, a woman who lived within two miles north of Vergas was sweeping her front porch steps and cleaning some rugs. Everything seemed perfectly normal until she took a rug and gave it a snap to shake the dirt off. With that noise, there was a sudden commotion beneath the porch, and out came a sasquatch, which had apparently been sleeping or hiding there. It immediately ran into the nearby woods, leaving behind one very frightened lady. I have no description of this creature, but one can assume it must have been fairly small to have fit into such a space.

The following winter, I was on the trails with my friend and fellow sasquatch enthusiast Dan Nelson. In the same valley where I had found the previous footprints, we found bipedal tracks in the snow leading into the woods, where we saw a branch broken seven or eight feet up. We followed the trail for a quarter mile or so before losing it near a small pond. A short time later, we saw a trapper walking along a trail nearby and decided the tracks were probably his. A disappointment.

However, another set of tracks turned up on August 10, 1990, and these were definitely not those of a human being. I was with Tim Olson this time. At the top of the same valley, on a gravel road, about ten prints were evident under the powerline. They came out of the ditch, went along the side of the road, then went back in. Some minor road maintenance was going on, and the prints were in fresh sandy gravel, deep and soft. In this unstable surface, the toes did not show up clearly, but the measurements were staggering.

The length was 20 1/2 inches. The width, eight inches toe end, 6 1/2 heel end, and again there was an apparent arch. (Actually, the science of biomechanics teaches that even a flat foot can raise a small mound of dirt in the middle of a print when stepping out, giving the impression of an arched foot, so this is not certain. Most sasquatch tracks seem to indicate a flat foot.) Also, there was some kind of lump behind the toes running lengthwise along the foot for about four inches. This was consistent from print to print. The stride varied but reached an astonishing 84% inches. Whatever made the prints, it was BIG, and standing where it had stood, I found myself looking up to try and visualize it. It couldn't have been the same animal that made the earlier tracks, which were "only" 16 inches long. Two Hairy Men?

Down in the valley, we found wild raspberries growing, a possible food source, although something that big would have to eat an awful lot.

Tim was less willing than I to accept that a sasquatch was involved, but we monitored the spot that night. Nothing showed up.

A couple of weeks later, I went back to the spot. There were no new tracks, but one of the old ones was still there in deteriorated condition. I also found some freshly broken tree branches.

On May 27, 1992, I started feeling very glad I had discovered that powerline valley.

The author (above) and Tim Olson (below) show the stride (up to 84 1/2") of tracks they found in Vergas Trails on August 10, 1990. These tracks measured 20V long.

While alone, I found another track, and this one made me recon-
sider something I had seen back in my earlier days of searching
Vergas Trails.

On March 31, 1989, I had seen a strange mark in a snowdrift a
short distance down the road from the valley. This mark looked like a
footprint with only two toes. It was about a foot long, six inches wide
at the toe end, and tapered to a very narrow heel only about 2½
inches wide. But there was only one print, and in an open area like
that, there should have been more, so I dismissed it at the time as just
a random scuff mark of some kind, not an actual footprint at all. I had
some bad luck with it anyway. While I was crouching on the edge of
the drift to photograph the print, the snow suddenly collapsed, and I
fell on it, completely destroying it.

Then in May of 1992, I was making a casual check of the valley (as
I still continue to do) when, just a few feet down from the road where
the 1990 tracks had been, I found another footprint in a narrow patch
of soft earth between patches of tall grass. It was 12 1/2 inches long,

four inches wide at the heel, and six inches wide at the toes. It was about 3/4" deep, and this time the fact that there was only one print made sense. The track maker would have stepped only once on this section of soft earth. And the number of toes? Two.

There was one toe on each side, with what may or may not have been a very slight impression of a third or partial third toe in the middle. The print curved substantially (one might even call it bent) and appeared to be that of a left foot. In the grass in the direction of travel, it looked like there may have been a slight trail.

The similarity to the strange mark of 1989 was striking, the only major difference being a slightly wider heel. I rather had the impression of a foot with missing toes, such as from frostbite or some other natural misfortune, rather than one that was designed for only two. I also wonder if this might have been the creature that the Vergas woman encountered hiding under her front porch in 1989, although I have nothing to back that up other than the small size.

There was still one more tantalizing discovery to be made in that valley area, and it came on June 11, 1993. I was there with a friend, Alan Weaver when familiar tracks turned up in two different spots not far apart.

What appeared to be the largest creature's track (the one from August 1990) was found going down the steepest side of the valley. It was about 21 1/2 inches long, eight inches wide at the toe end, five at the heel, the toes unclear but showing just a bit of heel drag as if the animal had slipped while going downhill. Actually, it was more of a scuff mark than a footprint, and if that had been the only find, the day would not have been all that exciting (unless you count the fact that at one point, I was attacked by red ants).

But then, a short distance down the gravel road from the top of the valley, it appeared that the medium-sized creature had put in an appearance along with its larger companion. It was Alan who spotted the prints, quite old, in a sandy ditch bottom beside the road. Due to recent rains, most of the animals' trail had been wiped out, but enough remained for us to cast one print measuring 16" long, eight inches wide at the toes, five at the heel. That cast is nearly a perfect match for the one I made in August of 1989, with only slight variations in width, and one cannot help but think that the two tracks came from the same animal.

Scuff mark going downhill, found on June 11, 1993, possibly made by the same creature as made the 1990 tracks.

Footprint showing only two toes found on May 27, 1992. The knife is 11 1/2 long.

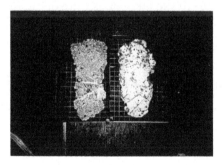

Two 16" casts that appear to represent the same animal. The one on the left was made on August 31, 1989, the other on June 11, 1993.

On the left is the forepart of a cast of one of the 20 1/2 tracks from August 10, 1990 (the rest was broken). On the right, the two-toed track from May 27, 1992.

Fifty-two inches to the right and facing in the same direction were the remains of two prints 20" long, ten inches across the toes, and 6" at the heel. These prints were perfectly side by side as if the animal had stood still there. It had obviously been some time, however, since anthills had been made in the print of the right foot, and we surely would have missed them if Alan hadn't first spotted the 16" track. The clearest impressions in the large ones were of the toes, which may not have all showed but numbered four per foot as they were.

Something is still making tracks in Vergas Trails after 25 years. I don't know if they are there all the time or if they only stop there occasionally, but they are real and alive, and there appears to be at least three of them, so perhaps the legend of the Hairy Man is not yet at an end.

The powerline corridor at the north end of Vergas Trails where a snowmobiler may have once seen the "Hairy Man" walking atop the ridge and where many footprint discoveries have been made.

5

HERE, THERE & EVERYWHERE - THE NORTH

This chapter is going to ramble a bit, I'm afraid, as it will cover several widely separated areas throughout the upper half of Minnesota. Basically, this will be a collection of reports that just don't fit well under any other heading.

Let's begin with a reference to chapter three, in which an article in the International Falls *Daily Journal* mentioned the experience of Chipper Lowe and another person in an unspecified year. The article dealt mainly with Koochiching County, but this particular incident, in which what was thought to be a sasquatch shook a trailer with people inside, occurred to the south near Marcell in the Chippewa National Forest. This forest is roughly 60 miles long by 50 miles wide, quite an extensive wilderness that lies right in the center of the state's northern half. I have not been able to meet Chipper Lowe but his neighbor, DNR agent Harvey Cole, says Lowe is sure it was a sasquatch he encountered, and his is not the only report from the smaller of Minnesota's two national forests.

Ed Trimble heard about a man, initials M.A., who reportedly saw a huge manlike footprint in a muddy place far back along an old logging road in the Cass Lake-Turtle River area. It was said to be very long and very fresh, and he could see such details as the fine lines in the sole of the foot and the toes (dermal ridges). He brought a friend in to show the print to and intended to come again to take pictures and/or make a plaster cast, but it was rained out before he got the chance. Again, the date is unknown.

Another Chippewa report also comes to me by way of Ed Trimble, who interviewed Sheryl Riggs, who now operates a small grocery store near his home in Clearwater County. Her experience occurred between Leech and Cass Lakes when her then-boyfriend was driving her home on a night in early November of 1971. Here is a partial transcript of the taped interview:

SHERYL RIGGS: ...It was cold outside, there was a little bit of snow on the ground... It was about ten, ten-thirty at night... It was a long, windy gravel road that we were on... We were driving along, we rounded a curve, and I was looking out my window to the right when my boyfriend said, "What was that?" ...We zipped right past it, then we stopped. And what we had seen when we were rounding the curve... I believe he must have seen it first because he was driving and I was looking out the passenger window... was this tall white thing... It was at least six feet tall, if not taller. It ran across the road in front of us, it paused by the edge of the trees, and turned and looked at us, and I remember distinctly that one arm was— the left arm was in front of it, and the right arm was behind a little ways. Now, we zipped past it, and we stopped, and we couldn't believe what we'd seen, we weren't sure what we'd seen. And I remember it moved very smoothly when it went across the road, and it was white. All white. Smooth looking. We turned around and went back to his parents' resort and told them what we'd seen, and they kind of were joking around, and they said no, it must've been one of those lumberjacks running around in his long johns. I didn't know what to think of that, in the beginning of November, what kind of lumberjack would be running around in his long johns. But we were pretty scared, we stayed there overnight. I remember it to this day, seeing that creature, whatever it was, standing by the edge of the tree looking at us. His eyes did not reflect the light, that I remember.

Cass Lake may turn out to be a promising area, for still another report from there serves as our final one from the Chippewa National Forest. While on a Native American spiritual retreat, my friend Alan Weaver heard about a woman with the initials C.N. who, with a friend, had seen a sasquatch in a swampy area near Cass Lake. Other details are lacking on this case so far, such as the date and any description of the creature beyond "big and hairy," but the witnesses apparently became frightened and ran away.

Moving east, we come to a report that has the distinction of having been at one time the only one on record for all of Minnesota in the popular literature. This, of course, was before any research had been done in the state to uncover any others.

On November 12, 1968, Mr. Uno Heikkila was hunting deer ten miles north of Floodwood. He was sitting on a stump when he saw a strange creature about 4 1/2 feet tall jump down from a balsam tree 125 feet away and begin walking off on two legs. Heikkila wrote to the famous investigator Roger Patterson of Yakima, Washington, saying that he thought it was a child at first, but then he realized it was "something I had never seen before." He followed it for about 200 feet but lost it in the forest.

Slightly northwest of Floodwood is the small town of McGregor.

I heard from researcher Mark Hall that sometime before 1970, road workers there are supposed to have glimpsed sasquatches along area roads fairly often. Unfortunately, I have been unable to uncover any further details on this.

I have another brief reference, in Steiner & Warner's *Minnesota Bigfoot News*, to two creature sightings in the vicinity of the town of Outing. No details are given, but the writers say they went to the area on June 2, 1978, to explore the woods, apparently finding nothing.

A much more detailed report comes from that same region, coming to me in a letter from one of the witnesses, initials B.P. It occurred at Aitkin in the summer of 1976, the witness being 14 at the time. One day he and a friend, R.G., were riding their bikes along an earthen dike that runs along the Mississippi River on the northern edge of town. B.P. wrote:

"It was about 8:30 p.m., and we both had to be home at dark, so we took off along the top of the dike for home. At one particular spot on the dike, there is a large swampy area approximately 300-500 yards across between the dike and a narrow row of trees that border the river. As we rode by this area, we noticed a large brown animal out in the boggy area. We thought it looked like it was digging in the swamp grass or picking it. We watched for about a minute, I guess, it didn't seem to notice us.

"Then I hollered at it. It was then I realized it wasn't a bear. It stood straight up and looked our way. It didn't have ears that stick up or a long nose like a bear. Then it turned and took off running, just like a man would, on its back legs, toward the river. It scared the hell out of us, and we took off riding as fast as we could. I wasn't afraid until it stood up and took off running. We then rode back to my friend's house and told his older brother what we had saw. He didn't believe us, but we rode back down there, and didn't see anything. The next day, we went back there, and we were going to walk out there and look for tracks, but that particular area was really swampy. The first step on the very edge was about 6-8" deep in water and muck. It may have been different where this thing was standing, but I doubt it. It was probably worse, and yet it ran across this stuff like it was dry pavement. I am an avid hunter, and have had to cross areas like this before, and no way could I run through this stuff like this animal did. It was not a bear. I don't know what it was. But I will never forget it. To me, this was something unexplained. I am not sure what I saw, but I think it was Bigfoot."

In a later letter, he added:

"...the height I would estimate at between 5'5" and 6'5". The ground was very soggy and it looked like he was sinking in the mud as it moved. I said he, not knowing what sex it was, figuratively. It looked rather thick and husky, rather muscular- maybe 300 pounds.

"The face was hairy, like a full beard and moustache, really full. Long arms that reached to the ground to pull up weeds easily. It was in long weeds, so hard to see legs and tell how long they were.

"...The area north of Aitkin is mostly swampy area, many lakes, rice paddies, and limited agricultural area... A lot of logging north of Aitkin.

"I do believe that there could be several families of these creatures that could live in the area, and no one would ever see them. The terrain is [a] thick wooded area, swamps, and wild. Perfect cover."

I like that report very much for its details in describing what the creature was doing and what it might have been eating.

Taking a big jump across the state to the northwest, we now come to Graceton, near the Canadian border. This report came to me from investigator Ray Crowe of Portland, Oregon, who heard it from Darrel Bulzomi, police chief of Bingen, Washington.

In 1978 Bulzomi's son David was at a crossroad near Graceton in Minnesota when he saw a sasquatch cross the road. It stood taller than a nearby road sign and was described in simple terms as "real big". Two weeks later, a tracker was taken to the scene and found footprints.

Further details on that sighting are lacking, but in 1976, the same or at least similar creature had been seen by a boy in his front yard just three to four miles away.

Moving south about 130 miles, we arrive in the area of Bemidji, a popular Minnesota tourist city with its gigantic statues of Paul Bunyan and Babe the Blue Ox.

The 1969 book "The Abominable Snowmen" by Eric Norman contains a report, date unknown, of a sighting within the city itself. Norman writes:

"K.R. (initials used at his request to protect anonymity) keeps a bait shack in Bemidji, Minnesota. One night, as he tells it, '...I woke up to hear this godawful ruckus in my minnow tank. My dogs were howling and barking like all

Billy-hell. I snapped on my porch light and let out a yell. That's when I saw

this big, black hairy monster tear away from the minnow tank and head for the woods. I sure as hell am glad that I didn't get in its way. It would have plowed me under."

The local Indians, as you may recall from chapter one, are

supposed to know all about the sasquatch, and the creatures' presence in the area into more recent times may have been indicated by the sighting of a mysterious something in August of 1987.

Lisa Deiderich of Fargo, North Dakota, attended El Lago del Bosque (Lake of the Woods) Spanish language camp (not to be confused with Lake of the Woods in extreme northern Minnesota) near Bemidji when she was 15. While out walking to the restrooms one night, she suddenly encountered a huge manlike figure walking just off the path she was on, very close by. It was up to seven feet tall with a powerful build, but she saw it only in silhouette and couldn't make out any other details in the darkness. She was quite frightened by the incident, as can be expected, and needless to say, there was no one that big at the camp that it could have been that she saw.

The next day when she described what she had seen she was told, "It must have been Bigfoot!" This was said quite seriously, as there were apparently stories going around about the creatures being in the area.

There is one more Bemidji story of a most dramatic nature, told to researcher Marion Senn by an acquaintance named Mr. Plautz. This is almost identical to another incident told to her from Koochiching County (see chapter three).

In November of 1993, Mr. Plautz was hunting deer with his two sons about 18 miles north of Bemidji. Near dusk on their first day out, he had returned to their Ford F150 pickup ahead of the others and sat down in the vehicle with his rifle to wait for them.

He was shocked by the sudden movement of the pickup as its back end was physically lifted off the ground. Seconds later, the whole vehicle began to be bounced violently back and forth, and Mr. Plautz was thrown about inside the cab. Looking back, he saw a huge, hairy manlike form, eight to ten inches taller than the cab, standing there gripping the truck. Its color was a chocolate brown. The attack went on for upwards of three minutes, during which time the frightened man kept a firm grip on his rifle in case he needed to defend himself against a direct assault from the creature. He was also concerned for his sons, who were still out in the woods.

Finally, the creature dropped the truck and fled into the woods. The shaken hunter watched it leave and was most impressed with the length of its stride. It left tracks 17-18" long, which were five feet apart.

Mr. Plautz and his sons had a day left of their hunting trip, but they cut it short.

Farther south, in Hubbard County, is the scene of another report from the Eric Norman book:

"In a letter to the author, a young scoutmaster told of having seen a manlike creature of enormous size while canoeing with a group of Boy Scouts on Mantrap Lake in northern Minnesota.

"The thing came out of the woods and walked to the edge of the lake,' writes E.G. (initials used at his request to protect anonymity). 'It glanced up at us, the boys became frightened that it might charge us. It was a monster! It had to be fully seven feet tall and broader at the shoulders than any pro football player. It was covered in long, black hair, and at first, I thought that it must be some massive gorilla that had escaped from a zoo.

Mantrap Lake in Hubbard County, the scene of the Boy Scouts' encounter.

The gorilla theory just doesn't work, however. This thing had buttocks, and its arms were in better proportion to its body than a gorilla's, that is, the arms were not so long.

"After the initial shock of seeing the incredible beast emerge from the forest, the boys seemed to relax a bit and to take in the wonder of it all. Everyone had stopped paddling, as if the sound of paddle striking water might frighten the beast back into the woods.

"The creature stooped to suck up some water and it drank like a workhorse on a hot day. Every little while it would stop to glance up at us, then it would move its head back down to the lake's surface.

"'When it had finished drinking, it just looked at us as stoically as a cigar-store Indian. Its features, although largely covered with hair, were definitely human, but yet I am certain that it was not a man. I mean, it was not a man such as we are. What was it?'

"What was it indeed?"

In a comment on this, Olive Rentfrow of the Hubbard County Historical Society had this to say:

"...a neighbor's son who was in the Scouts remembered a story once told around the campfire one night: Two loggers, one quite short and one unusually tall, were working in the general territory of Big Mantrap lake, and were caught one night in a bad thunderstorm. The lightning struck the taller and knocked the other one unconscious. When he came to, he could find no trace of his companion, and never did find out what had become of him. But it was after that that folks began telling of seeing this oversized person or creature who looked very much as you described it from the scoutmaster's account. This may or may not have been true, or just a product of someone's imagination. It's the best I could come up with... Some of us are as curious as you. It would seem that there must be more to all these stories, wouldn't it?"

I think we can safely dismiss the idea of these two tales being in any way related.

My friend Dan Nelson used to work at Camp Wilderness, the Boy Scout camp at Mantrap Lake. Although he never heard either of these stories while there, he believes the area is very suitable to hide a large number of sasquatches. He, too, has seen much of it by canoe.

(There is an interesting ghost story told at Camp Wilderness that Dan related to me, the tale of "Big Red." Red was a hermit, a large and hairy man whose cabin sat decades ago on the ground that is now the Scout Camp's archery range. The cabin was destroyed in a forest fire, and Red went up with it. However, soon afterward, and perhaps still today, his ghost began appearing in the area, roaming the woods. And in his wake, he left small piles of ashes in the bottoms of gigantic manlike footprints.)

We come now to one of my favorite reports, so considered because I was able to personally investigate it at the scene relatively soon after the incident occurred and because it involved that rarest of all sightings- multiple creatures. The witness wishes to remain anonymous, so I have given him the pseudonym Steve Carter. He would

also like the exact location kept secret, but it is in Becker County, where I happen to have spent my childhood and had a sighting of my own.

Early on the morning of November 4, 1990, Steve Carter was hunting deer near the small town where he lived. At about six a.m., he was sitting in his pickup truck atop a small hill overlooking an area of woods and swampland locally known to contain many deer and a few moose. Some distance off to the right, he thought he could see another hunter concealed in some foliage, though it was still somewhat dark.

About half an hour passed with no signs of movement. A little more light had begun to creep in over the horizon, but the sun had not yet completely risen.

Suddenly Steve heard movement in some thick brush down below to his left, and he prepared himself to get his deer.

Despite the woods' thick shadows, he was then able to make out a vague shape within the brush, but now he was puzzled. He saw a large, low down dark object about six feet long, and beneath it, moved more than four legs. It didn't seem to be a deer, and it wasn't. When it got to the edge of the trees and emerged into a small field of tall grass at the bottom of the hill, Steve got a shock. He saw that it was not one animal but three moving together.

What Steve saw was a trio of two-legged manlike creatures

roughly the size of human beings, one slightly smaller than the other two, walking quickly in a stooped-over position, low to the ground in a stealthy manner. The small one was in the center. There was not enough light to make out specific details of their appearance, but their outlines were clear, and it was obvious that they were all covered with dark hair, not clothing. Their heads were roundish in shape, their arms nearly touching the ground in their stooped positions.

The creatures moved along the bottom of the hill less than a hundred feet from Steve's truck, then reached a point directly in front of him and turned sharply to their left, increasing their pace across the grassy field to disappear back into the woods on the other side. At no point did they straighten up.

Amazed, Steve went down to examine the site. Three trails of flattened grass were clearly visible where the creatures had walked. Once the initial shock of seeing the mysterious beasts had begun to wear off, he started to think seriously about what he had viewed. He assumed the small one had been a juvenile; thus, they were probably a family group. It also occurred to him that they may have been traveling in such a stealthy manner to avoid being spotted by the other hunter stationed nearby.

Seeking corroboration for his sighting, after a time, Steve went over to talk to the other man. He did not mention specifically what he had seen, just casually asked if the man had seen anything. The reply was negative. Apparently, the creatures had been successful in hiding from at least one pair of eyes that morning.

It would have been nice to be able to examine the scene of the sighting immediately, but as it happened, Steve did not contact me for some time, and it was

November 30th before he took me there. Interestingly, though, the tall grass in the field was frozen and so still clearly showed the trails of the three creatures. Directly in their path were some gopher mounds that had some vague scuff marks in them, but other than this, we found only deer and moose tracks.

I returned to the site on December 16th, alone this time, for a more thorough search of the surrounding area, which took nearly three hours. It was a good day for it, as we were having a very mild winter up to that point, and only a light dusting of snow covered the ground at the time. I wanted to walk the creatures' path and try to work out where they had gone and where they had come from, possibly to find some footprints somewhere.

Upon approaching the hill, I saw an encouraging and somewhat surprising sign: three side-by-side trails of flat grass identical in appearance to the original trail were visible along the side of the hill. It was impossible to tell what had made them, of course, but they were intriguing. First, I went to the spot where the creatures had gone back into the woods on the far side of the field. It didn't take long to lose the trail there. Almost instantly, I was in a tangled mess of brush and undergrowth. A short distance in, there was a small stream that cut through the foliage and led to the nearby swamp. Perhaps they had walked in the stream, I thought, where the going was easier, so I made my way to the swamp. It was frozen solid, however, and no tracks were about to show up on solid ice.

For a long time, I walked through the woods from which the creatures had first come, much thinner than the dense growth across the field but still thick enough to provide shelter. I found four tree stands in different locations, used by hunters to get the drop on deer. One happened to be extremely close to where Steve had first seen the creatures, and it was obvious that they had to have gone right past it, but if the stand was occupied on the morning of November 4th, no one has come forward to report seeing anything.

Finally, there was the very spot where the creatures had emerged from the woods, and there I found something very interesting. Tree branches up to an inch thick were snapped off at three distinct heights: 65 inches, 74-76 inches, and 83 inches. They were still slightly attached, just hanging by a thread as if something had taken them in hand and given them a quick jerk sideways. Since the sighting had occurred six weeks previously, it was too late to tell if these breakings were fresh enough to have been made on that day, but this find was interesting to me for two reasons. First, for the particular spot where the broken branches were, and second, because I had seen the exact same kind of breaking in Vergas Trails (see chapter four). Branches can bend and snap under a heavy wind, of course, but with this particular type of breaking, there was no other damage around the snapped branches to indicate wind. Rather, it seems very selective. I can not say for sure that the sasquatch does this, but it seems possible.

A close look at this photo shows the trails of flattened grass left by the three creatures seen by Steve Carter.

On the left is one of the broken branches at the spot where the three creatures emerged from the woods. Compare this to a young healthy birch sapling snapped off at a height of seven feet in Vergas Trails (right).

Steve Carter thought the creatures he saw had probably just been passing through the area and were not permanent natives, and I tended to agree with him. The woods there were not large enough to hide or support them for very long, and the surrounding territory was all wide open farm land. One thing puzzled me, though. Why had they come out right in front of Steve's pickup when it was clearly visible on the hilltop? The answer may lie in the fact that farmers sometimes leave trucks, tractors, and other machinery sitting out in fields overnight or longer, and wild animals can become used to seeing them and not always associating their presence with that of human beings. (There was a spot nearby along the wood line where several old rusted machines had been left to scrap.)

Whatever the case, this report is a good example of how sasquatches can and do pop up where you least expect them.

In fact, on April 28, 1994, one did it to me again!

From the small community of New York Mills in Otter Tail County comes another report told to me by Marion Senn, and this one is firsthand as she was lucky enough to experience it herself.

The exact location of the sighting was County Road 67 just outside Heinola, which is little more than a wide spot in the road a few miles from New York Mills. The area is made up of farmland and scattered woods, some swampland.

Just after 9:00 p.m. on a Thursday evening, Marion was driving toward her home when she saw a large figure suddenly come into view on the road ahead of her. She described it as a manlike creature about seven feet tall with a big upper body and a very short neck, a fairly rounded head, and thick, dark rust-colored hair such as she had never seen on any other animal. The legs and arms appeared somewhat darker than the rest of the body.

As she drew nearer, the creature took only two steps from the center to the edge of the road, bent down at the knees with its arms back, and leaped off the road down into a small boggy area mostly covered with trees where she lost sight of it. She guessed this leap would have been nearly 20 feet freefall.

As it happened, this bog was right next to the driveway of Marion's neighbors, Ed and Florence Kasma. In an excited state, she drove in to tell them what she'd just seen. The next day Ed went out to have a look around.

There were no true footprints anywhere, but impressions of flattened grass were found both on the opposite side of the road from where the creature had leaped off and on the far side of the bog, leading out of the trees into an alfalfa field for about 20 feet along the treeline and then going back into the bog. These impressions were 16-18" long. Where the trail re-entered the trees, there were small branches snapped downwards in two opposite directions at a height of about *AH* or five feet, as if the creature had parted them.

On July 16th, I was able to examine the scene of this sighting.

The snapped branches were still to be seen, and I collected one as evidence. These breakings were much like those in the Steve Carter case but featured scratches that could have been made by the creature's fingernails.

Marion also happened to know of another encounter that took place in the early or mid-1970s, only about three miles away.

The scene of the April 1994 sighting near New York Mills. The arrow shows where the creature was standing.

The barn where Verna Kyrkyri encountered a sasquatch.

A lady by the name of Verna Kyrkyri lived alone on an out-of-the-way little farm on the opposite side of Heinola from where Marion's sighting was. One day some noisy chickens first alerted her to a disturbance in her small barn in which she kept some tame rabbits. Upon investigating, she was startled to see the back end of a large hairy animal stooped over in the barn. It was scrambling around trying to catch a wild cottontail that had wandered in, but naturally, Verna was concerned about her cage full of tame rabbits as well. She took the intruder to be a large bear.

Verna ran and grabbed a broom, then returned to the barn and went inside to drive the bear out. Being a rather slight woman, according to Marion, it is hard to imagine her having the courage to take on such a challenge, but with an angry slap, she struck the bear on the hindquarters. Only then did she discover that it was not a bear at all but a two-legged creature that had been unable to stand fully upright under the six-foot ceiling of the barn. Apparently not wanting a fight, it fled from the barn and ran to a nearby swamp.

I have examined Verna's old farm, now abandoned and overgrown with weeds. There is still a rabbit hutch in the sagging barn, sitting there in the cramped little arena where old Verna Kyrkyri once took on a sasquatch and won.

Finally, it seems a shame to have to wrap up this exciting chapter with something rather anti-climactic, but a brief trip in July of 1995 led me to the Galaxy Resort on Star Lake near the small town of Dent. It was rumored that some strange animal had recently come through their cabin/campground area, "stinking badly." Foul smells, of course, are a well-known trait of the sasquatch, and patrons at the resort were supposed to have complained. There were no other details available, so my first thought was "skunk," but could a mere skunk smell cause such a stir? (Funny man David Letterman put it best, I think, when he said, "Skunk isn't exactly the worst smell you'll ever smell, but it's certainly the most smell you'll ever smell.") Plus, this area is quite near Vergas Trails (approx. 15 miles), so on Wednesday, July 19th, I decided to drive over and check out the rumor.

But when I talked to the resort's owner, he knew absolutely

nothing about it and was quite amused with the very idea of sasquatch. The Galaxy Resort is small, with just a few cabins and campsites, and is surrounded by fairly open areas- farmland, etc. Star Lake is quite large, and fishing and waterskiing are popular there. It is hardly what I would consider sasquatch country despite the forest 15 miles away.

The originator of the report turned out to be the local mailman. I'm not sure where he got his information, but all in all, I had to mark this one down as highly unlikely. I'm sure skunks, though, do live in the area. (And most people would rather run into a sasquatch!)

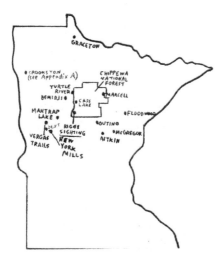

Map showing locations of reports in the north.

6

MILLE LACS LAKE

In passing, I heard once from Mark A. Hail, who studies anything and everything under the sun that's unusual, that there has supposedly been some type of monstrous creature reported to live in the waters of Mille Lacs Lake in Aitkin and Mille Lacs Counties in the mid-eastern part of Minnesota.

There is, of course, an entire category within cryptozoology that deals with creatures like this. They range all the way from little-known examples like this all the way to what is probably the world's most famous monster of any type, Scotland's Nessie. Similar to, but also different from the oceanic "sea serpents," these fresh water beasts have appeared in lakes around the world and have often been given amusing names by the local people. Lake Okanagan in British Columbia has Ogopogo, while Lake Manitoba emulates him with Manipogo. In Lake Champlain on the New York-Vermont border, the local monster is known as Champ (and there, by the way, is one promising investigation).

So what should we call this mysterious denizen of Mille Lacs? I know- Millie!

If this animal exists, it must not appear nearly as frequently as some of its more famous cousins, for I have no other references to it.

The lake is more than big enough for it, though, spanning 25 miles long by half as wide, much bigger than Loch Ness.

But this book is about the sasquatch and whatever lives beneath the surface of Mille Lacs Lake. I am aware of three reports of something equally strange seen on its shores.

In July of 1989, when I was touring southeast Minnesota, I stopped in La Crescent to look into a sasquatch sighting there by a duck hunter in 1968 (see chapter eight). I found no official record of it, but as I was inquiring at the local police station, I ran into one of those odd coincidences that just occasionally happen. The officer on duty, Ron Morris, had himself seen a creature up at Mille Lacs in the summer of 1974.

The sighting had occurred when Morris was still a teenager. He filled out the following report for me:

"While driving west on hwy. #27 I observed a light/medium brown 'creature' standing on the north shoulder of the highway. It stood on two legs and had the same basic form as a human. It was covered with hair that appeared to be two or three inches in length. The arms may have been longer than that of a human. It stood approximately five to six feet in height."

The sighting was at about one a.m., and the creature was standing in low swamp land beside the lake. Morris said he thought it weighed about 150 pounds.

Sightings by law enforcement officers are always of special importance. They are trained observers, expected to be completely accurate when making reports. Even though Morris was not yet a police officer at the time of his sighting, his hindsight after his training remained clear as to what he saw that night. Having a reputation to uphold, I was impressed at how he volunteered this story to a total stranger.

Officer Morris said that he also knew of a woman in the same area, initials S.A., who had seen the same or a similar creature at about the same time and place, between the towns of Isle and Wahkon near Izatty's Resort on the lake's south shore. In fact, he said, she had even been chased by it. However, inquiries to this woman brought no response concerning the incident in question.

When an investigator like myself can come up with reports like these just by casually poking around, it makes one wonder how many more such stories are out there waiting to be accidentally discovered.

Tim Olson came across another sighting report from the Mille Lacs Lake area, one of a more recent date. He wrote the following account after interviewing the witnesses:

"Two Minnesota men reported seeing a Bigfoot-like creature during the first week of July 1989, on the N.E. side of Mille Lacs Lake in Aitkin County, Minnesota. It was about 5:30 a.m., and the two (Brad and Greg) were walking back to camp near the lake with a full moon out. As they were walking, the two noticed there was apparently something following them on a wooded ridge above them... Both men thought the curious animal to be a bear... When they reached camp, they noticed some movements on the wooded ridge, and as they watched, a human-like figure was standing in clear view between two trees... It was about 75 to 100 feet away... The creature stood upright, had long legs, narrow hips with its arms hanging down to the knees, and it stood about eight feet tall. Its eyes were round, and it had hair on its head and body except for the facial area. Its nose was flat, and it had little or no neck. The color of its hair was a dark brown. It had a huge chest and shoulders. The creature seemed curious and unafraid... It made no moves or gestures, and after about three minutes of observation, it slipped into the shadows and trees and disappeared."

One of the men also commented to Tim that the creature looked somewhat like the one in the movie "Harry and the Hendersons."

I can't help being struck with the irony of the fact that I was just a little to the south of this area on a sasquatch expedition at about the time this happened!

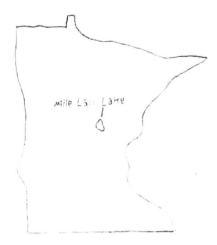

So far, these few reports make up the extent of known sasquatch activity around Mille Lacs Lake, but who knows what the future holds?

7

THE SOUTHWEST - A SOLITARY SNOWMAN

The southwestern part of Minnesota is nearly a blank on the sasquatch map. It lacks the dense forests that are common to other parts of the state and does not have as many lakes as most other regions. Thus it makes sense that the creatures would not find it a suitable habitat.

I know of only one report from the southwest, actually a small group of sightings from the community of Windom. Located along the Des Moines River, it is a fairly small city of fewer than 5,000 people. I learned from Mark A. Hall that in the winter of 1966, it was the scene of several sightings of a large white-haired sasquatch, but unfortunately, I have been unable to learn anything more about this.

A letter to the Windom Chamber of Commerce produced the following reply:

"We have no information on Bigfoot sightings in the Windom area. This is a very interesting request, and I would be interested to get any information you might have on a Windom Bigfoot... Good luck with your research."

They provided me with the addresses for the local newspaper and police, neither of whom responded to my queries, so there the matter will have to rest for now.

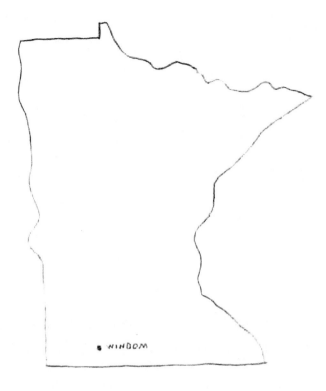

WINDOM

8

THE SOUTHEAST - BLUFF COUNTRY

One of the most famous areas in sasquatch lore is northwest California, an extremely rugged country containing steep, rocky bluffs covered with nearly impenetrable forest growth. The descriptively named Bluff Creek was the scene of Roger Patterson's famous 1967 film of a living sasquatch.

There is very similar territory, although on a much smaller scale, in southeast Minnesota. Bluffs and regular forest land make for some of the loveliest scenic views in the state, especially along the Mississippi River, which forms the border with Wisconsin and is the single biggest factor in this region's geography.

The terrain is not all that the region has in common with northwest California. Several sasquatch reports have originated there.

First of all, the book "The Abominable Snowmen" by Eric Norman tells of a series of sightings around Winona in December of 1968. I looked into this, however, and found that this was probably confused with an escaped criminal named "Bigfoot" Johnson, who had size 18 feet and was hiding near the city at that time. Not an encouraging report, but there are plenty of better ones.

The same book had a report from the fall of the same year, not far down the Mississippi near the town of La Crescent. A man with the initials J.L. had a duck blind in a swamp and was hunting with a friend. As he told it:

"My friend had gone back to the car to get his pocket warmer. As it is quite a walk from the road to where I have the blind, I was surprised to hear him come clomping back so soon. It sounded like he was trying to stomp in his footprints so hard the grass would never again grow where he walked."

I poked my head out of the blind and yelled: 'Bill, you jughead, quiet down, or you'll scare the damn ducks back to Canada!' Well, sir, I found myself looking right in the face of something that had to have come full-dressed from an alcoholic's d.t.'s. It was black and hairy and big enough to take on the Green Bay Packers' defense. It had been kind of stooping along the ground like it had been looking for roots or something. When it stood up, it just didn't want to stop!

I stand six-three, and this thing left me staring at about the middle of its chest.

"I didn't know what it was, but I knew I was scared. The dad-blamed thing looked like King Kong. I don't really remember pulling the trigger of my shotgun, but I do know that I was <u>not</u> aiming at the creature. It just looked too manlike.

I mean, it looked more like a man than an ape or something.

"It let out a scream and took off for the trees. Bill was coming running down to the blind, and it took me four minutes and five cups of coffee before I could tell him what I had seen."

La Crescent police officer Ron Morris, who saw a sasquatch himself at Mille Lacs Lake in 1974 (see chapter six), told me that he didn't personally know of any such activity around La Crescent, but he added, "I've always thought it was possible."

Beware of a creature that can make a man down five cups of coffee in four minutes!

In either late 1968 or early 1969, dramatic events occurred near Rochester, one of Minnesota's major cities, home to the world-famous Mayo Clinic.

One night a student named Larry Hawkins was driving south from Rochester on Highway 52 bound for Decorah, Iowa. Near midnight, he suddenly saw a figure crouched at the roadside. Thinking someone needed help, he pulled over, but then in his headlights, he saw that the figure was an apelike creature covered with hair and with thick shoulders. It stood up and ran from the road, up an embankment into some woods, and Hawkins got out of the car. He found that the creature had been crouched over a dead rabbit. Examining it, he found no blood; thus, he guessed it had not been killed by biting. (More likely that it was roadkill.) At that moment, he heard a sound from the woods, described in different sources as either a roar or a "harsh bark of protest." Frightened, he drove away quickly and reported the sighting to police, who did not take him seriously.

At about the same time, and possibly the same highway, a trucker who drove an early morning route from northern Iowa to Rochester claimed that he often saw "monkey men" standing in the road. His fellow drivers laughed at his story, but they changed their minds when the man's rig overturned at about 4:30 one morning. He was killed in the accident. It was thought that he may have been trying to swerve to miss one of the strange beings.

A third Rochester report, this time at the edge of the city itself, occurred a decade later on December 14, 1979. Three days after the event, the Rochester *Post-Bulletin* ran the following account:

WOMAN CLAIMS SIGHTING CREATURE ON AREA ROAD

Has the legendary "Bigfoot" come to Rochester?

An unidentified woman told Olmsted County sheriff's officers Saturday that she saw a beast that would certainly match descriptions of a creature reported in the northwestern parts of the United States over the years.

The woman refused to give her name for fear of criticism and reported the incident only as an effort to allay the fears of her children, who also saw the beast.

The woman said she was returning home Friday night with her children, who are two and three years old. On the road between Rose

Haven and Marvale additions, her headlights suddenly picked up a huge beast.

She described the creature as being 7-feet tall, 250 to 300 pounds, covered with hair, and having a huge mouth, with a pig-like nose, and "very ugly."

"It was definitely not a man," the woman said.

She also said the creature attempted to cover its eyes from the glare of the headlights, and "the arm did not bend like a normal arm."

Sheriff's officers could find no trace or tracks of the creature.

I've been on the road in question, and despite being within city limits, it does have considerable tree cover.

Back closer to the Mississippi again, two 1976 reports from the Rushford area came to my attention through Mark Hall, who received them in a letter from Terri Burt of the La Crosse, Wisconsin *Tribune*. Describing the experience of a local woman, Burt wrote:

"She was alone in her rural home early one evening when her dog began barking, growling, and/or groveling in apparent fear. Armed with a small-caliber pistol, she, alone in the house, opened the door a crack and saw a pair of reddish eyes and smelled a foul odor. She immediately locked the door but continued to hear 'it' rummaging around outside the house and heard its strange wailing cries. She did not actually see what was making the disturbance...

"Also, my correspondent in that area tells me that a sighting was made in that area about the same time and two unidentified boys from Lanesboro, Minn, got some kind of casts of prints at the time."

It is not made clear whether or not the two boys who made the casts were the ones who actually had the second sighting.

It was also in this region, you may recall, that the mysterious events on the Prarie Island Indian Reservation near Red Wing occurred (see chapter one).

Finally, though, I should bring up a case that almost no one (including myself, I think) takes seriously. In 1971, researcher and scientist Ivan T. Sanderson received a letter stating that a sasquatch-type creature had been captured after being found digging through garbage bins in the Minneapolis-St. Paul area. It was supposed to be being kept at the Rochester State Hospital, where it refused to wear clothes and had to be thrown food because it was too wild to approach.

There are wooded areas along with the river system in the Twin Cities, and some researchers believe sasquatches may use rivers to travel around, but still, I doubt this story has any truth in it. I tend to think someone may have been trying to play a practical joke on Sanderson in the wake of the publicity surrounding his involvement in the infamous Minnesota Iceman case (see chapters 19 and 20) which was also in southeast Minnesota.

And we will get to that soon enough.

The road in Rochester along which the December 14, 1979 sighting took place.

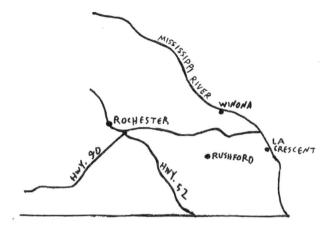

Map showing locations of reports in the Southeast.

9

CARLOS AVERY - WHAT IS GOING ON HERE?

I n the early '1970s, a very annoying trend began to infect the sasquatch field. Particularly in eastern states (but actually everywhere), cases began to appear that involved not only the usual creature sightings and track finds but also UFOs and other forms of paranormal phenomena.

There were reports of apelike creatures being shot but then vanishing in a flash of light as flying saucers hovered nearby. Some people claimed to have received flashes of psychic communication from the creatures they saw, such as has been reported in many contacts with extraterrestrials. Single cases involved such bizarre details as an apparent sasquatch seen walking with a glowing sphere in its hands and footprints found with grass in them that was flattened and spiraled in the same way as the crop circles that have gained such attention in recent years. Some even claimed to have seen creatures inside or emerging from UFOs, and their behavior continually seemed to indicate that the sasquatch was either from another planet or from some unknown parallel dimension, that they were not flesh and blood animals at all but something supernatural.

Many investigators, myself included, would be very happy if these reports would somehow go away and leave us alone. They are freaks within a mystery that is already strange enough, and they do no one any good. If the creatures are so intangible, after all, then they will remain elusive forever, so all of us might as well just give up right now. Many of us have chosen to ignore these reports, to put as much distance between them and us as possible, for skeptics are quick to point out how they seem to discredit the entire sasquatch issue. However, this is unfair and unprofessional. If we claim to be impartial, mustn't we listen to such reports openly in the same way we do to a "normal" sasquatch report? After all, the people doing the reporting are just as confused as we are, in the same way as someone who has done nothing more than find giant footprints or see a hairy creature running through the woods. Ignoring something just because it does not fit our preconceived notions is exactly the kind of thing we have been complaining about ourselves in this field for so many years.

Thankfully this kind of thing has not been widespread in Minnesota, but it has reared its head a couple of times, notably on the Carlos Avery Game Preserve about 30 miles north of St. Paul. The case was thoroughly looked into by private investigator Bradly Earl Ayers and also involves another strange phenomenon that has been linked to UFOs, animal mutilation.

This bizarre series of events began in 1971 on a farm within the area. The family involved has remained anonymous. At that time, mysterious lights were first seen floating over the property. Then more sinister things began to happen; livestock, including a calf, a horse, and some pigs, were killed by an unknown intruder that tore off their heads and completely drained their bodies of blood. The same thing happened to a deer carcass that had been hung in a tree during hunting season. This activity went on sporadically for a few years.

The farmer reached a point where he had had enough. He carefully
prepared the ground around his farm in an effort to detect the killer's tracks but to no avail. Whatever it was continued to visit the farm without leaving a single footprint.

Eventually, the farmer and a neighbor began staying up all night with loaded guns in hand, determined to confront the strange nocturnal prowler. What they were not at all prepared for was the glowing cylindrical UFO that flew overhead on the night of August 18, 1976. They really did not know what to make of it, but what happened the next night was even more bizarre.

In the early morning hours, as the men stood watch, a piercing scream described later as a "screech-growl... half human and half animal" came from a nearby marsh. Minutes later, more screams were heard from several different directions at once. Whatever it was, there were quite a few of them. Then, finally, a dark form appeared over a rise. It was manlike in shape but much bigger. The farmer's watchdog, usually quite fierce when confronted with an enemy, ran for cover beneath the camper in which the men waited, and this sudden motion seemed to startle the creature. It retreated, uttering another scream as it entered the marsh.

Nothing further happened for a few months, but when the next hunting season arrived, the men were puzzled to discover that all the deer, so plentiful in earlier years, had vanished. It was the first year that neither man made a kill. A seeming explanation came when the farmer's brother rushed home from hunting in a panic one day. Something had followed him through the marsh, he said, something huge that stayed just out of sight behind trees but uttered blood-curdling screams if he got too close to it. The farmer himself went to investigate, and he, too, encountered the mysterious stalker. The men decided it would be wise to stay out of the marsh from then on.

I have looked into this story a little. The most recent animal killing recorded by Ayers was in April of 1977. A letter from the local sheriff's office assured me that "All is quiet on the Carlos Avery Game Preserve," although they admitted to being aware of the past events. Mark A. Hall, however, tells me that he's heard things have still been going on down there in more recent times.

Generally, I do not involve myself in the investigation of UFO reports. However, it is a field I have great interest in, and I enjoy keeping up with all the latest news relating to it. It has received a lot more attention in our culture than cryptozoology ever has, undergoing intense scientific scrutiny and involving our government at its highest levels. Reports of encounters with alien beings are so prevalent now, I don't think there's any doubt that there is indeed an extraterrestrial presence on Earth, but while I find this a fascinating subject, I do not have the time or resources to investigate everything. Sasquatch research is time-consuming enough, and I am quite content to leave UFOs up to others, but when they intrude on the sasquatch field, they do force me to form an opinion as to what is going on.

I have never believed that the sasquatch is anything but a natural red-blooded part of Earth's fauna, and it will take a revelation of astronomical proportions to make me change my mind. Now, if a UFO and a sasquatch happen to show up in the same place at the same time, calling it a coincidence might be just a little too easy. So what else might be happening?

Consider this: The study of abductions by alien beings shows that aliens have an intense interest in the human race, regardless of what their intentions might be with us. Might they not also then take an equal interest in the animal that most closely resembles man, even seek to understand why man seems to refuse to believe in this animal? Alien interaction with the sasquatch then becomes much easier to understand.

There is also another possibility. I once read an account in which someone had seen a group of large black dogs come running out of a landed UFO in a graveyard. The impression given was that these were not normal dogs, not that all black dogs must come from another planet. So, by the same token, when a creature seems to display unearthly qualities but still looks basically like a sasquatch, isn't it possible that there is a form of alien life out there somewhere that, either by design or coincidence, just happens to look an awful lot like our hairy friend? This theory could be complete rubbish, or it could be right on the money, but whichever, it's unlikely that we will know for sure any time soon.

Thankfully, the vast majority of sasquatch reports put the creature firmly within the realm of earthly zoology. It conforms perfectly well to all the laws of nature and physics 999 times out of a thousand.

When dealing with extraterrestrials, no one on this planet is really qualified. There is so much room for limitless theorizing that it's possible for none of the investigators to have the correct interpretation. But with our sasquatch, somebody's got it right.

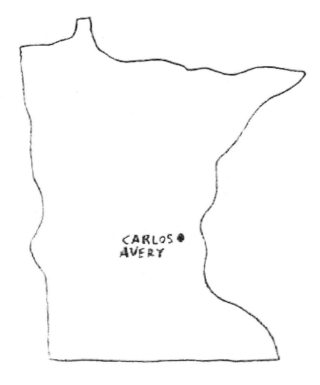

10

HOAXES

There are a lot of skeptics who would have people believe that all or most sasquatch reports are the results of hoaxes, deliberate attempts to fabricate evidence and pass it off as real for whatever peculiar reason holds value in the mind of the perpetrator.

It's a truly unfortunate circumstance that such hoaxes do indeed occur, and they can have a very damaging effect on the sasquatch phenomenon's credibility. Some people have gone as far as to construct artificial giant feet to lay down fake tracks or even to dress up in ape suits and jump out at unsuspecting witnesses, but the easiest (and therefore, the most common) form of hoax is simply to make up a story and present it to the public as convincingly as possible.

It's important to examine the hoaxes as thoroughly as the genuine reports so that we can learn to tell them apart. Minnesota is fortunate not to have been plagued with this problem to any great degree, but a few nasty little episodes have occurred.

There was an alleged attack by an unknown creature on a young man near Fairmont, just ten miles north of the Iowa border in southwest Minnesota, in late November of 1978. This has sometimes been interpreted as a sasquatch report.

According to the *Fairmont Sentinel*, shortly after midnight on a Monday morning, 19-year-old David A. Tonne went out looking for animal tracks near Center Creek north and west of the George Lake Dam near Fairmont. He was searching for a good spot to go hunting. Suddenly he heard a strange noise (undescribed) and aimed his flashlight at it, but he saw nothing.

Moments later, with his flashlight in his pocket, he heard the noise again and turned to face it. He then heard a brief growl an instant before something "very large, taller than he, somewhat furry" struck him from out of the darkness. He was knocked down, falling backward and onto one knee, but managed to balance himself on one hand and was up again quickly. He turned and ran without getting a good look at the animal.

Tonne's ski jacket was left with five "clean cuts" on the right side and sleeve, and two on the left, presumably scratches. Two of the scratches went through to damage his flannel shirt, and one made it through to the skin, marking his chest slightly.

Three Fairmont policemen, two Martin County sheriff's deputies, and the chief of police from nearby Welcome investigated at the scene. The ground was very muddy, but they found only numerous deer, raccoon, and human tracks along with several "distorted and unidentifiable tracks" in the mud. Investigations were begun to determine what sort of "ill, injured or otherwise dangerous animal" had attacked Tonne.

When I first heard about this case, I was unsure if a sasquatch or a bear might be the culprit but tended to lean more toward a bear because sasquatches are practically never described as having claws. As for the newspaper, their headline read "Police Probing Reported 'Animal' Attack," with "animal" in quotes as if they suspected something unusual about the attacker's nature.

As it turned out, however, I learned later that the whole story had been a hoax. The Fairmont police found that the "scratches" in the coat had been made with a knife, not the claws of any animal.

What could motivate someone to make up such a story? Perhaps just a simple bid for attention.

Then there are a couple of peculiar cases from around the city of Fergus Falls in Otter Tail County. Despite being a nice, charming little community, this city is often on the receiving end of some very bad jokes because it happens to be best known as the home of a state mental hospital.

In looking for information on the Vergas Trails "Hairy Man" (see chapter four) in 1990, I contacted county sheriff Gary A. Nelson. He had nothing on file about Vergas Trails, but he did have this to offer:

"I was with the Bureau of Criminal Apprehension for 25 years... I have personally investigated two similar episodes (one in Fergus Falls and one in Todd County), and both were unfounded, and each of the many persons who claimed to have seen 'a red-bearded giant' later confessed to being party to a hoax. Large numbers of police officers, National Guard, and Reserve units had been activated before the hoax was uncovered."

Sheriff Nelson apparently had only a very limited idea of just what the sasquatch is supposed to be. In talking with him later, I learned that this "red-bearded giant" was described as a huge, demented human being but had actually been invented as a fictional scapegoat when a security guard on the grounds of the state hospital made some clumsy mistakes and wanted to avoid embarrassment. Later some other people used this character in a bogus report to authorities, again to cover for something they themselves had done wrong.

Something similar happened in June of 1992 when the Fergus Falls *Daily Journal* printed this brief but tantalizing bulletin:

"BEAST SIGHTED: Some residents of Newton Township have reported seeing a 6-foot tall upright beast with long hair hanging around farms. They also reported that clothing has been missing from clotheslines and produce missing from gardens in the area, according to the Otter Tail County Sheriff's report."

This got some peoples' attention, and the report was widely repeated in the radio news. I went to Fergus Falls to check it out, and the real story turned out to be quite ordinary. The "beast" was quite human, probably a transient, and had been reported as such.

Although he had long hair, he had been described right down to his clothing, so there is no chance that a sasquatch was involved. This seems to be an example of the liberal media deciding to have some fun with an otherwise mundane story.

But the granddaddy of all newspaper hoaxes in Minnesota happened on April Fool's Day, 1991.

Early that month, I received a surprise in the mail one day. It was a newspaper clipping describing a most remarkable sasquatch incident up in the Arrowhead region of Minnesota, the great boreal forests north of Lake Superior. The sender was Jim Schneeweis of the Department of Natural Resources in Grand Rapids. I recognized his name from the 1979 article on sasquatch tracker Richard Johnson (see chapter three) and was flattered by the fact that I was becoming well known enough in the state for the DNR to contact me.

Now, I am not implying that Mr. Schneeweis was aware of the true nature of the story at the time, but in any case, here is the article he sent me:

MAN-BEAST SIGHTED, TRACKED ABOVE HOVLAND

It was just after dawn Friday, March 22, when DNR forester Orvis Lunke headed up the Arrowhead Trail north of Hovland. A storm the night before had left the road slippery with wet snow, so he began slowing down when he spotted the dark form ahead.

"At first, I thought it was a moose," he said, "but when I got closer, I could see it was walking on two legs."

Lunke said he came to a stop about 100 feet behind the animal, which was walking away from him along the road.

"It wasn't a bear, but it was walking upright," he said. "It was covered with shaggy, red-brown hair. It was really scruffy looking."

In moments the creature strode a short distance down the road, turned, and cleared the snowbank in two steps. Before entering the woods, the creature stopped and looked back.

"I'll never forget that look," Lunke said. "That hairy thing looked me dead in the eye, and it had a face like a man's."

Lunke noticed the animal was the same height as a nearby balsam sapling.

Then it strode into the woods through two-foot snow.

"That snow hardly slowed it down," Lunke said. "The snow didn't even come to its knees."

Lunke leapt from the truck and ran down the road to where the beast entered the woods. He couldn't see the animal but could hear it crashing in the brush.

He listened until the sound faded into the distance. Then he examined the tracks in the fresh snow along the edge of the road. The five-toed, humanlike tracks were nearly twice the size of his own boot prints. The stride was over five feet.

Lunke considered strapping on his snowshoes to follow the creature but decided it was best to get help. He went back to his Hovland office and called DNR wildlife manager Bill Peterson in Grand Marais.

"Orvis didn't tell me over the phone what he'd seen," Peterson said. "He just said there were some fresh tracks I should see."

Peterson drove out and met Lunke in Hovland. Together they went up the Arrowhead Trail to the site, which was just beyond Irish Creek.

"I started laughing when Orvis showed me the tracks," Peterson said. "I thought he was pulling my leg."

But Peterson stopped laughing when he followed the tracks to where they crossed the snowbank and entered the woods.

"It appeared that it would be difficult to fake tracks like that in deep snow," Peterson said. "Then Orvis told me he'd seen the darn thing."

The two men used a Polaroid camera to photograph the prints. They laid an axe alongside a track for comparison. The print was almost as long as the axe handle.

Then they measured the balsam sapling Lunke had determined was the same height as the beast. The sapling was nine feet tall.

"The tracks went right past the base of the tree," Lunke said. "I'd say the animal was the same size."

The pair decided to follow the beast, which was headed east toward the Swamp River basin. They needed snowshoes to travel in the deep snow.

"It just headed straight into the woods," Lunke said. "The tracks were easy enough to follow."

The beast stayed in thick cover and seemed to prefer traveling through dense balsam stands. It walked as if with purpose, the men said, never meandering or appearing to stop.

"I told Bill the only way we'd catch up was if it bedded down someplace,"

Lunke said.

In one place, the men discovered a tuft of reddish brown fur on a branch above their heads. They took a photo of the fur and then collected it as a sample. The hair is currently being analyzed by a team of experts at the University of Minnesota.

"I'd expect we'll have results in another week or two," Peterson said. "So far, all they've told me is that it's puzzling."

Eventually, the tracks led to the open marsh meadows along the Swamp River.

As the men approached the open area, they heard a commotion in some willow brush ahead. They watched in stunned silence as the beast emerged from the brush and lunged across the meadow toward the river.

"It was mostly going on two legs but occasionally dropped down to all four," Lunke said. "I was so surprised I forgot to get a picture."

The creature broke through the river ice but plunged across. When the water reached its waist, the beast began swimming.

"I guess a dog paddle would be the best way to describe the stroke," Peterson said.

When the animal reached the far side of the stream, it soon disappeared in the willows. The men followed to the river bank but were reluctant to cross the bad ice.

"By the time we found a place we could get across the ice, we'd lost about an hour," Peterson said.

They quickly resumed tracking. After following the beast for three more miles, they emerged on the Otter Lake Road near Prout Lake. The creature had crossed the road and headed into the Pigeon River Valley.

"It was getting late, and we were several miles from the truck, so we decided not to go on," Peterson said.

On the way down the Arrowhead Trail, the men talked about their strategy for the next day. They considered contacting the Sheriff's office, but the beast had committed no crime. Instead, they decided to call in a DNR airplane. However, the weather foiled their plans. A severe rain and snowstorm raged through the night. The airplane was unavailable the next day.

When the pair returned via snowmobile Saturday morning to where they'd left off the chase, the tracks were nearly obliterated.

"We were able to follow them about a mile further, but then they were mixed in with moose tracks, and we lost them," Lunke said. "The way the weather looked, we decided to give up."

Heavy snows fell Saturday. When the storm ended, the "Swamp River Monster" had vanished. Subsequent aerial flights along the Pigeon River revealed nothing. However, the two men decided it was best to tell the story to *News Herald* readers.

"I've never encountered anything like this before," said Peterson, "so I can't assure people this creature is harmless. Apparently, it hasn't bothered anyone so far."

This wasn't the first report of a manlike beast in the Swamp River country. Others have trickled into Peterson's office during the past year.

"Last fall, a bear hunter from the Twin Cities came in and said a 'bigfoot' had approached his bait," Peterson said. "At the time, I thought the guy just didn't know a bear when he saw one."

Other reports have included strange calls heard at night. Several campers at nearby Esther Lake last summer said they heard ape-like noises in the forest near the campground.

"I don't like to speculate," Peterson said, "but the animal we saw crossing the river was like none I've ever seen before."

A sasquatch hunter could hardly ask for a better report. It truly had everything: corroborative testimony from two credible authority figures, physical evidence, and a very recent date. I was tremendously excited and made plans to make the six-hour trip to the Hovland area to try picking up the trail.

Perhaps I should have realized, however, that it was just too good to be true. I wrote the witnesses to see about arranging to meet with them, and Bill Peterson sent the following reply:

"Thank you for contacting me regarding the newspaper article. Unfortunately, this was published on April 1 as an April Fool story. The last paragraph contained that statement. However, when the regional office receptionist clipped out the story, she inadvertently left off the last paragraph. As you can imagine, this caused quite a stir in the regional office. A number of telephone calls were made to this office, and they eventually found the missing paragraph; but apparently not before you had been sent a copy of the incomplete article.

"Sorry to get your hopes up over this since you do have a serious interest in these matters. I must admit that I feel there could well be such beasts in the western U.S. but am skeptical of reports in the mid-west."

I believed what Peterson said, but just to be thorough, I had to confirm the untruth of the story. It wouldn't have been the first time that authority figures had hastily tried to cover up such a story when it started to result in unwanted attention. However, both the editor of the Cook County *News Herald* and the biology department at Duluth's University of Minnesota did confirm that the only truth in the story was that Lunke and Peterson and all locations named do exist.

I was disappointed and angry at the fact that this kind of thing can so easily happen in the sasquatch field when so many people do not take it seriously. Even though this particular hoax was all for fun, I was not very amused.

It has often been my experience that even when covering a genuine sasquatch report, the press tends to treat the subject so lightly that their account ends up being riddled with inaccuracies and slanted in a humorous direction. Apparently, since the reporter may not believe in the creature in the first place, they don't think this matters. I don't mean to condemn all papers everywhere because there has been some excellent reporting done over the years, but the problem does come up often enough to make me rather uncomfortable. A large (probably the largest) part of research into the sasquatch phenomenon depends on old newspaper stories. If a big percentage of those stories are inaccurate, it's no wonder there are so many misconceptions about the creatures. It is this kind of thing that helps keep the whole issue in the dark year after year.

Therefore, when doing research, read the accounts with a careful eye for detail and use common sense in your interpretations. Always confirm the stories with the actual people involved whenever possible. And if something sounds just too far out, it probably is.

Some documentation of the Hovaland newspaper hoax.

PART II

THE ADVENTURE OF CLEARWATER COUNTY

CLEARWATER COUNTY

I first became involved in the sasquatch activity in Clearwater County in early 1991, and it was this more than anything else that made me start to think I might really be able to accomplish something as an investigator. Nowhere else have I been so impressed with the amount of firsthand evidence (both in the form of eyewitness accounts and more tangible things) that I've been able to obtain. There isn't another spot on the Minnesota map with such a dense concentration of reports, and leads obtained in this area have even led to other parts of the state.

Much of this I owe to Ed Trimble. Prior to December of 1990, when he was 76 years old, Ed never gave much thought to the sasquatch mystery. Now it is a big part of his life, and I'm very lucky to be able to call him a friend.

If Ed and I are right about what is going on up there, then we have made some very significant discoveries. I almost feel guilty to be such a relative newcomer to the field and yet be on to something so important, but I can only present the facts as I have found them to be. A situation existed, and I just happened to be the one that was there to pick up on it.

What I believe we are dealing with in Clearwater County is evidence of two different species of creatures- closely related, both being what we would call "sasquatch," but clearly separate- sharing the same land. There are other areas in North America where more than one species has been reported, but here it really seems that we may have a type that has not been described anywhere else.

The reader should be aware that a lot of criticism has been laid on this case by people who firmly state that if the footprints do not conform to what we have seen before, then they can not possibly be a sasquatch. Ed himself, being somewhat of a social activist, has been very outspoken and tends to stir up controversy at times, and the critics of his story are entitled to their opinions. However, I truly think they are missing the point, as they so often do, and that point is this: Even if there is only one species of sasquatch in existence, we still have on our hands here something unidentified that walks on two legs, something definitely cryptozoological no matter what you wish to call it, and that in itself is a major discovery.

Time may yet tell who is wrong and who is right about Clearwater county. You be the judge.

11

PUZZLING TRACKS

I tasca State Park in Clearwater County is famous as the home of Lake Itasca, the source of the mighty Mississippi River. It lies in a typical Minnesota wilderness region, covered with dense deciduous and coniferous forest growth and containing many kinds of wild animals. It's a beautiful area in which I have camped and thoroughly enjoyed myself. (Some people mistakenly think the park is actually in Itasca County, but that county is farther east.)

Mr. Ed Trimble and his wife Nova live about nine miles from the north entrance to Itasca Park, near the tiny community of Zerkel and just down Highway 200 a short distance from a recreation spot called Long Lake Park. Now getting on in years, Ed has lived an exciting life in the great outdoors. He has worked as a professional hunter and trapper, mainly going after trouble-making predators like black bear and timber wolf, and has also kept beehives that are sometimes raided by bears that must be dealt with. Years of such activities have made Ed as close to an expert on wildlife as you are ever likely to find among the general public. Spend time with him, and you will hear many thrilling tales of events witnessed and predators conquered. He may bring out the huge bear paws he has stored in his deep freeze.

Likely as not, Ed will also tell you of his distaste for wildlife officials like certain DNR agents he could name. In years past, he was a bit of a political activist, arguing with them over many issues, primarily the current lack of bounty that was once paid on predators. He feels this has allowed their numbers and depredations to increase to dangerous levels despite the DNR's claims that the animals are actually threatened.

Ed is often skeptical and wary of authority figures in general after a number of negative experiences. He has in his possession two geological specimens of unknown type which, he feels, "cannot be explained by recent or current theory as to how such were formed."

Many years ago, he contacted the Smithsonian about them, but despite the potential importance he feels they may have, he has received no reply. On another occasion, in 1953, he sighted a mountain lion near his home and reported it to the DNR, but they proceeded to discredit his story and insist that mountain lions do not exist in Minnesota, even while looking right at the big cat's tracks. (I and other cryptozoologists know that the lions do indeed still survive in the midwest, and in fact, Ed reports that they can still be seen and heard occasionally around his home.) "For this and other reasons," Ed says, "cannot trust or respect them."

It comes as somewhat of a surprise, then, that Ed decided to report the finding of what he felt could be sasquatch tracks on his property. He and Nova thought it their duty to report, regardless of the consequences.

He enjoys going for walks on and around his land just to be in the out-of-doors and to observe nature, and this is what he was doing on December 9, 1990, when he walked past the garden behind his house, through the rows of small trees he tends to, and out to the medium-sized man-made pond a couple of hundred yards from the house. The weather had been unusually warm for some time, thus, there was no snow on the ground to speak of, but a dense, even layer of snow half an inch deep covered the ice on the frozen pond. There, just off the bank, were some tracks that the long-time tracker and trapper had never seen before. Despite all his experience, he could not identify them, and they made him deeply puzzled.

The tracks were roughly oval in shape and showed only two toe impressions. Where the other three should have been, there was what appeared to be an impression of hair growing <u>under</u> the toes, a most unusual feature. ("Snow in this area mushed up as though by coarse, heavy hair," Ed wrote.) Between the visible toes was a sharp-edged ridge of hard-packed snow.

Following are parts of a detailed four-page report I received from Ed in early February 1991. It included careful tracings of the strange tracks. As he writes, they were of two different sizes: the larger 8 5/8" x 7 1/8", the smaller 7 3/4" x 5."

"The larger creature's prints were more nearly round but otherwise the same.

It stayed very close to the edge and didn't stride over 24." Slid its foot for 12 or 14" before putting full weight on it as though being careful. Lengthened stride before long and stopped sliding foot but still stayed right by the edge.

Signs were that this creature is quite heavy, the weight and/or warmth of pad (including toes) melting the snow. Prints very distinct with clear-cut edges. The smaller one came on ice about 20' later than the larger one but ventured further out. They were on the ice for a distance of about 47 yards. There were no other type tracks such as a creature 'going on all fours' would leave."

At first, I suspected bears, but Ed was quick to point out that the tracks showed no claw marks and no gap between the toe and foot pads, not to mention the fact that they appeared to be those of <u>two</u>-legged animals. Whatever these creatures were, they were not bears.

Ed continued:

"There was no snow left on land or in the woods at that time. Prints weren't fresh enough to arouse our dog, who has a pretty good nose. Came back, got [my] wife and camera, took snapshots.

"...Shortly before this time, we'd had a thaw. We think that these prints were made while the temperature was at least in the 30 above range and conditions ideal for prints on a snow-coated, solidly frozen pond.

"We are in the second year of drought, and the pond is at its lowest point.

It loses some through seepage, so the ice near the edge has a slant to it. This might account for the larger one staying so near land.

"We would not shoot such rare creatures unless they prove to be very dangerous or destructive.

"...I am 76 and have been interested in science, natural science, hunting, predator trapping, wolf snaring, and outdoor observation most of my life. I've seen my share of bear, wolf, and cougar and their tracks, but this is the most unusual, weird, and unbelievable thing I've ever seen in the way of tracks.

"...We hesitated to tell anyone about this mostly because the type of toes and their placement seems so weird, plus the fact that the creatures apparently walked upright. But then we decided, what have we to lose? I was steered to Harvey Cole at Northome, MN, and he gave me your addresses (this report was sent to both myself and my associate Tim Olson). We were glad to hear of you."

I was pleased to see the mention of Harvey Cole's name. Knowing of his involvement in the sasquatch scene up in Koochiching County (see chapter three), it was nice to know he was still interested.

Ed concluded his report with a description of his area and some conjecture:

"We are in the wooded hills... past Itasca State Park and Clearwater County Campgrounds through which angles the continental divide. To the northwest are several large farms devoted mostly to beef or dairy cattle and feed for same.

Well over half the area is timber, sloughs, lakes, and small streams... To the east and south, the lay of the land is much rougher, and there are few permanent residences and no farms for many miles. It would appear to be the glaciers' dump grounds. There are many small lakes and bogs, much-mixed timber, and few roads.

There are acorns, hazel nuts, June berries, blueberries, a few strawberries, and, rarely, mountain ash. Chokecherries are more dependable, next is acorns.

"Large creatures that don't hibernate and can't survive on twigs, bark, and buds would almost have to be predators or scavengers to survive here. It appeared that the tracks paused at a beaver patty. (He thought the creatures might prey on beavers.)

"...That someone could be pulling a stunt on us— I think it's very unlikely but, if so- I'd have to laugh and say it's a good one!"

I made the trip to the Trimble home on February 10th. I spent several hours discussing the find with Ed and examining the cut-out paper tracings he had made of the tracks. I found him to be very interested and curious about the sasquatch issue in general.

We agreed on one very puzzling fact: although the tracks were definitely not those of any known animal, they also did not resemble the type of humanlike footprint usually attributed to the sasquatch. Still, what other conceivable type of creature could have been responsible? The sasquatch is the only denizen of our woods that always walks upright on two legs, and these were not the only tracks in the phenomenon's history that did not conform to the usual pattern.

Mark A. Hall has explained to me his belief that there are actually several different types of creatures in America that can be labeled "Bigfoot" or Sasquatch. Thus, the ones that visited the Trimbles' property could have simply been one of the lesser-known types.

Ed was intrigued when he heard of Steve Carter's November 4th, 1990 sighting, about 40 miles to the southwest (see chapter five). We both wondered if the same creatures might be responsible for his tracks. After considering this, he decided it was possible that there had been three, not two sets of tracks on the pond. The possible third set he had taken to be made by the smaller creature doubling back. It was a possibility but impossible to prove.

Apart from becoming convinced that something unknown had made the tracks, I also got a feel for just how wild an area this was. Animal populations were very high, especially predators. Other area residents, as well as Ed, described seeing and hearing mountain lions prowling about. Ed reported having recently seen two timber wolves running down Highway 200, and he said there were so many bears around that it could be only a matter of time before someone was attacked. (In the summer of 1994, a man was injured by a black bear near Park Rapids, about 35 miles from Ed's area. The man had first shot at the animal after it had tried to get at some food stored inside a small cabin.)

Life had gotten very interesting since Ed's find. His wife Nova said that as she worked in the kitchen these days, she was always glancing out the window toward the pond, wondering if she could catch a glimpse of the mysterious visitors. Ed, meanwhile, had dreamed about them. After reading my first book, he would later write:

"Glad to hear of the white ones being seen. That's what I saw in my dream, you know... there they were huddled together in the woods about two or three hundred yards away. Wasn't a scary dream, but woke up before I could get close enough to make out details, but they were white as snow. I had no slightest inkling that anyone had ever seen white ones or even that any serious study was on here. But, too many times, such dreams or hunches or whatever have turned out to be exactly true... too often for me to ignore. There has been times I should have paid more heed to the strong feeling I sometimes get... just a once-in-a-while thing... can't explain it."

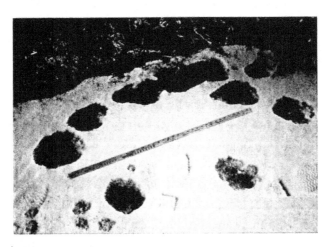

The Dec. 9, 1990 tracks, photographed by Ed Trimble. Note size in relation to yardstick and to human and dog tracks. Note also the place along the shore where the creature's foot has slid.

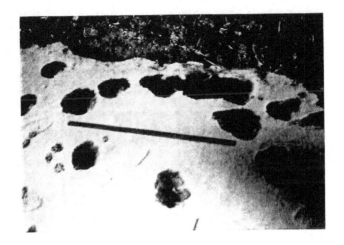

Ed Trimble. And the pond on which the strange tracks first appeared.

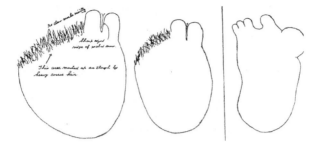

Figure 1- Ed's sketches of the large and small footprints he found on Dec. 9, 1990, measuring 8 5/8" x 7 1/8" and 7 3/4" x 5" respectively. Both of these are right feet, which means the large toes are "on the wrong side." This was the most amazing feature to Ed. Figure 2- Outline of a yeti footprint found in November 1951 on the Men- lung Glacier by mountaineers Eric Shipton and Dr. Michael Ward. It measured 13" x 8". Ed believes the creatures responsible for his tracks were similar to a yeti-type. There are differences, of course, but then the Shipton track is itself unique even in the annals of yeti lore.

12

THE VISITOR RETURNS

After Ed Trimble went public with the story of his discovery, quite a lot of attention came his way. He had placed copies of his report in many public places in the area, including in the town of Bagley to the north, the largest town in the immediate area. Reactions were varied. Some people were amused and suspicious, but most people who knew Ed took him quite seriously, given his well-known knowledge of animals and their tracks. There were even a few who revealed that they, too, had experienced strange things in the area over the years.

Ed's story was featured in three local newspapers. The Bagley *Farmers Independent* had a large front-page article under the headline: "Clearwater County man says tracks made by bigfoot- Did legendary creature leave its imprint in the snow in area near Long Lake Park?" The article stated:

...If Trimble is attempting to pull a practical joke on the community, it would be an act which defies his known behavior.

Kim Fultz, who lives a few miles from Trimble, said he's not known as a man to pull practical jokes.

"I've known Ed a long time. I don't think this is a practical joke...

He's been a trapper all his life. He knows tracks. I'm inclined to believe him."

Fultz had seen large tracks last winter when cross-country skiing near her
farm.

"They were so huge and scary that they made me turn around and go back home," Fultz said. Her son figured the tracks were probably made by a big bear.

(I have met Kim Fultz and her son Clint. After seeing Ed's tracings of the tracks, he had found she apparently said that what she had seen the previous year looked very similar. Clint, meanwhile, did not go out to see his mother's discovery but had seen bear tracks in the area recently and assumed she had seen the same thing. He is actually quite interested in the sasquatch mystery. There were also stories told of actual creature sightings- see later chapters.)

Such was the situation, then, on March 25, 1991, when Ed again went for a walk in the woods and came across more mysterious tracks, this time in very large numbers but apparently made by only one creature.

In a pasture adjoining Ed's property are two small water-filled potholes in a wide-open area surrounded by forest through which a few rough-cut logging trails wind. Considerable snow had fallen since his earlier find, but on this day, the temperature rose to 60 degrees, and at about 3 P.M., Ed walked toward the pasture to see if the potholes were melting and overflowing down toward his own pond. On the way, he stumbled across the new tracks. (Later, he would recall that his dog had been raising quite a commotion that morning.)

Over five inches of wet, heavy snow had fallen in the days prior to the warm spell, and this was the surface the creature had walked through. This time the tracks, though similar in appearance to the previous ones, showed a bit more detail. The two toes, which showed clearly at the outside corner of each foot, were spread wide apart, and there now seemed to be a very light impression of other toes along the rest of the foot, making tiny impressions only about the size of a dime. Ed commented that it reminded him of a photo of a yeti track he had seen, referring to the famous creature known to dwell in Asia's Himalayan mountains. Every other print also had an indentation in the middle as if the creature had a scar or growth on the bottom of its left foot.

The creature had skirted the edge of one of the watery potholes and then walked in a shallow ditch leading to the other one. None of its strides were over two feet long and in the ditch became very short, as if it had been walking cautiously or slowly. When it came to the other pothole, it turned away. Ed's impression was that it did not feel like getting wet in the icy water.

From there, Ed followed the tracks for a considerable distance through the pasture and surrounding woods. The creature seemed to have been wandering around aimlessly, and occasionally there were places where it had stopped to dig into the snow as if to catch burrowing rodents. Perhaps that was why it had been going so slowly, Ed thought. It was listening for the sounds of its prey beneath the snow, as do other predators such as foxes and weasels. At one point, the prints appeared to have toes on each end. This meant that the creature had backtracked and stepped in its original tracks going the other way.

Ed walked for several miles searching for more tracks but found only one place, further south, where the same creature had crossed a logging trail in the middle of the woods.

However, back near the pasture, there was a place where the creature had been within sight of Ed's house. It had come out of the woods and stopped at a small wire fence. There it had turned completely around several times as if unsure of how to continue, leaving large circular impressions in the snow. Descriptions of the sasquatch usually include an extremely short neck, almost no neck at all, so presumably, they can not turn their heads very far but must turn their whole bodies to view their surroundings. Finally, the creature had crossed the fence and continued on away from the house. Perhaps the barking dog had frightened it.

All in all, Ed estimated that he saw well over a thousand individual footprints that day and probably closer to two thousand. The snow was melting fast in the warm spell, so he quickly got his camera and took six photos, still marveling at the strangeness of what he was seeing. What struck him as oddest of all was how the largest toes were on the outside of the feet, the exact opposite of a human foot and of the more common type of sasquatch track. These prints looked much more yeti-like, and Ed continues to believe that is the type of creature that has visited his land. This one, he believes, was a young one, possibly abandoned just recently by its mother and/or father as many young animals inevitably are. This is the harsh way that nature teaches its children independence, and this creature seemed to be wandering around, unsure of what it should do. This is only speculation, of course, but it is very interesting and seems logical. Ed named this creature "Junior."

The next day Ed sprinkled some of the tracks with soil to make them show more clearly in the snow and photographed them again, but they had melted badly by that time and were a bit misshapen. Examining the tracks now, he came to the conclusion that they were probably not all made at the same time but over both the afternoon or evening of the 24th and the morning of the 25th.

Ed was tremendously impressed by this discovery. He saw an intelligence in this unknown creature that few other animals share.

The way it walked through deep snow, with short steps and occasionally walking in its own previous prints, suggested that it was consciously conserving its energy.

On April 16, 1991, Ed was interviewed by telephone on KSTP radio in St. Paul about the strange tracks he'd found. He recorded his own end of the conversation:

"It was a pleasant, overcast Sunday afternoon, December the ninth. I started out on one of my customary long walks. This time I was going to go through the

fields and hills and woods, and I got only about 350 yards from the house— I was

going across the surface of our frozen pond, which was covered with about a half-inch of snow— and I came upon these tracks that were very clearly made by a biped. One large one, and I think, two smaller ones. I have dubbed the large one 'Mama' and the smaller ones 'Junior,' and— these tracks were unlike anything I've ever seen pictured or ever heard anyone else tell of. I'm somewhat familiar with the stories about sasquatch and Bigfoot, and I've seen pictures of the casts of their tracks, saw one movie about it many years ago, about 20 years ago I'd say, and the tracks that we saw— I come back to the house and got the wife, and we went back down-- the tracks that we saw are entirely different. The large one's track's almost round, and its placement of the toe, the two toes, is what really set me back on my heels— it's hard to explain, but the two toes are on the wrong corner of the foot. The rest of the way, the snow was just mushed up, we thought as though by coarse, heavy hair. That's the way it looked to us, and that's the way we put it. We put 'as though,' those two words in there.

(Question on his reporting of the tracks) "...No, actually, that's where I goofed up. I didn't tell anybody for quite a while. And I didn't go down and cover these tracks with pieces of plywood or something like that as I should have. I did try to get some loggers that were going by to take a few minutes off and go look, I told them they'd never forget it if they did, but they were too busy making money and they didn't come soon enough. It snowed."

(Question on whether he has seen any other evidence) "...Well, I'm out quite often, in fact I've been out a while this morning already, we have snow here again now, and ah— I didn't really ever expect to see them again because I thought they were just passing through, and it's the first time in my life that I've ever seen anything of the kind, but on the 25th of March, I saw tracks of one of the small ones. In fact, he wasn't much over 200 feet from the house where he'd come across. There was a crust on the snow— the snow was about five to six inches deep at that time, and it had thawed and then formed a crust overnight. He was breaking through in some places, and this one was the one I dubbed 'Junior.'"

(Question on emotional reaction to the tracks) "... Well, no, I haven't been nervous about it at all. All the accounts we read of that type of creature are that they're quite shy when it comes to humans.

"...Well, when anyone sees one of them— now, all we've ever seen was the tracks, but others that I have come in contact with now and even in this area have actually had a glimpse of the creature, of one of the creatures. We think the ones that crossed our place twice now are more like the Y-E-T-I, the yeti, or I believe they call him the Abominable Snowman over in the Himalayas.

(Question on size of creatures) "... Well, the ones that they talk about out west and in the other places where they've seen the long-footed ones that have a track like a huge man track, they claim they get to nine feet tall, some people

say taller, and weigh possibly five to six hundred pounds, but it's hard to estimate, although I would say the large one of the three that we saw might weigh three or four hundred pounds according to the impressions made by the tracks.

"...Yes, I think the term 'Bigfoot' is a white man's all-encompassing name that he's applied to any biped that he can't understand.

(Question on skepticism) "... Well, not very much. Yes, I've encountered some who say they don't believe it because they haven't seen it. You always find that type of person, and one person in particular— I asked him if he'd been in the woods, and yes, he'd been in the woods a lot, and he was always interested in such things, and he don't even believe there's cougar in the country, and it's getting so now so many people are seeing cougar that you look sideways at somebody that don't believe they're here. (Author's note: A cougar was photographed by a neighbor of Ed's in the summer of 1991.) So he couldn't believe this because— or that there are cougar— because he hasn't seen it himself. Well, I said you said you've been in the woods a lot, and he said yes, and I said, well I can't believe that because I never saw you in the woods. So I turned it on him and set him to thinking, I believe.

(Question concerning the possibility of hoax) "... I thought of the possibility but then after we both looked at it and all, why we just about discounted that, and then since I've seen the single track here the 25th, why, I totally discount it.

"...It's a sign of intelligence. There's a little slant to the ice, too, because after it froze, the pond seeps a little, and that lets the ice down, and this could've caused the large one to be more cautious. I really think the only reason they went on the ice is because there was the faint lingering odor of beaver castor there on a beaver patty on the shore or near the shore. I think perhaps that they prey on beaver... Well, yes. Almost all animals are attracted to the odor of castorium.

"...No, I tell you, authorities and I, as far as the DNR is concerned, we don't get along very well... And I'll tell you one other thing that perhaps I hadn't told you before— after I sent that four-pager out, I sent it to Mike Quast in Fargo and to Tim Olson in Bloomington, and I sent it on Thursday from our rural mailbox, and there was a knock on our door at Sunday noon, and it was Mike Quast, and he spent the afternoon with us, and after he left the phone rang, and it was Tim Olson from Bloomington, and he kept me on the phone for an hour.

Ed's photos of the tracks he found on March 25, 1991. The following are his own notations about each photo:

CAUTIOUS. Short sidewise and forward steps when first going on grassed waterway, drifted full and with 1/2" crust ...thawing."

RETAKE. From opposite side and closer, part of No. 1. Note big toes spread for this type snow. See sign of lump or scar on one foot. This one is not heavy.

IT'S O.K.! Our Junior hasn't had too much to drink, he's on his way and can walk a straight line! Yes, this is one of the small ones. NO BATH! Junior leaves the 50 yd waterway between small, water-filled potholes in about the center of a hilly 15-acre pasture ringed by thousands of acres of wooded hills."

The day after his second track find, Ed took this photo of two tracks sprinkled with soil to show up well against the snow. By this time, however, melting and wind had distorted them considerably.

Junior's" view of Ed's house while making the March 25th tracks. The place where the creature crossed the fence is just out of frame to the left. The path leads to the pasture area, where tracks were abundant.

13

TROUBLE WITH THE PIGS

As Ed waited for his mysterious visitor to make a third appearance, he heard a number of stories from friends and neighbors who had had strange experiences as well. In a letter, he related the following story:

"Well, you wanted reports of unusual things. Personally, I think that Leslie Olson's story is about as unusual as you'll find... a very strange account of an awful big loss of 150 to 190-pound hogs on a farm about six miles from here on the east of the road to Bagley.

"Leslie Olson was in the little pig and hog business. He and his wife had been away for a few hours on this nice day in August of 1974. Upon returning, they knew something was wrong, for the hogs that pretty much had the run of the place were nowhere to be seen.

"Leslie investigated and found several of them cowering, huddled tightly together in the building they'd been raised in and shaking with fright. There was a storage room in the building with no door to the outside but one that closed from within. That door was shut and had to be broken down to see what was in this small room. 78 hogs had sought refuge in there and were piled several deep, their bodies had kept the door from opening. All of them had suffocated.

"The Dead Animal Service came and hauled the dead away to be processed into tankage, pet food, or whatever. No wounds beyond what one would think might be caused by their mad rush to escape whatever it was that frightened them was found on any.

"Leslie said that a neighbor not over two miles away said that an injured timber wolf went across their yard or lot that day... After checking up on the story with Leslie, I called him to get his account, but he says he does not recall the wolf.

"...Whether or not, I would have doubts as to a timber wolf putting that much of a scare into that many hogs, especially without wounding any of them.

"There was no dead ones outside, no blood seen, and no one found any wolf or bear tracks. However, I do not think that anyone made a thorough search, and I'm sure that the main desire was to get the dead animals off of the place before they got too rank.

"Sheep, cattle, and horses recover from a scare pretty quickly. As to hogs,

I do not know but am inclined to think that they would, too. I'd think that it took something absolutely hideous to frighten them so. I have raised a good many hogs here and in Iowa, and they seem to be quite stoic and, as Olson says, a whole bunch of men could not drive even half that many hogs into such a small room."

Of course, there was no sign that indicated the presence of a sasquatch in this case either. I have since met Leslie Olson, and he still says he honestly doesn't know what caused the tragedy. He never thought about a sasquatch, but Ed seems to suggest that possibility.

Would livestock react in such an extreme way to the approach of a sasquatch when other animals do not have nearly as much effect on them? It is possible. There are many stories on record of domestic animals becoming frightened when one of the creatures was known or believed to be nearby, and also of normally vicious guard dogs cowering in fear like little puppies in the creatures' presence. However, there are also reports of dogs attacking sasquatches and driving them away. Perhaps it has something to do with the animals sensing the creatures' intentions. Wild animals, especially those often preyed upon by predators, are very adept at knowing when they are in danger. Even domestic livestock that have lived their whole lives in fenced enclosures share this sense to a degree.

This case will remain a mystery, but whatever caused the sinister event, it was definitely something very strange.

Nova Trimble (right) stands with Leslie Olson and his daughters Sherry and Christie in the little room where 78 hogs died in a blind panic. One wall has now been taken out.

14

OTHER STORIES

Mysterious tracks were enough to conclude that something strange had made itself known in the Zerkel area, but since its tracks were so unusual, it was necessary to find eyewitness descriptions of the actual animal. Thanks to Ed, I found that such accounts were not lacking, and they actually made it sound as if the creatures had dwelled in the region for years. Not only that, but aside from the uncommon variety that had to be responsible for Ed's track finds, there also seemed to be the more common sasquatch with a humanlike foot present.

I found it amazing, as I always do in such a situation, that these creatures could exist in an area like this and remain unknown except for a handful of whispered stories among the local people. The fact that not just one but two species seemed to be present made the situation all the more intriguing, and so, between May 4-6, 1991, I decided to spend some time in the area searching the woods and talking to the other witnesses. Ed was happy to introduce me to these people, most of whom he knew well. He and I spent an afternoon collecting a number of interesting stories. Recounted here in chronological order are those and other reports that have surfaced from around the area.

One of the earliest accounts came from a man who wished to

remain anonymous. His experience had taken place in 1960 in the Buck- board Hills, a wild region just a few miles from where Ed had found the strange tracks. These hills happen to contain the second-highest point in Minnesota. It is also rumored, I am told, that DNR officials were aware years ago that the sasquatch existed there but were concealing that fact to avoid a mad rush of hunters. (This rumor has yet to be confirmed.)

The man, who I'll call Bob, had been logging in the hills and knew them well. One day in late October, he was out hunting near McKenzie Lake. It was about 4:00 in the afternoon, clear weather, sunny, with patchy snow on the ground in some places. Suddenly Bob smelled a very foul odor, "as bad as the waste lagoons at a chicken

farm." He then saw a strange creature about 200 yards away sitting on a windfallen log. (I wonder, however, if he hasn't overestimated that distance, as there are few places in those hills where one can see that far.)

The creature was about seven feet tall, weighed around 400 pounds, and was covered all over with fairly short brown hair, including its face. Its head was pointed on top. Its arms were about the length of a human's, its legs fairly long, its neck short but not overly so, and it had a stocky body. It was eating a fish, holding it in both hands. When it saw Bob, the creature let out a screech like that of

a lynx, jumped up, and, leaning forward slightly, ran away into the woods, dropping the fish. Bob saw that it was a male, for it had a prominent male organ about 12 inches long. (Although also mentioned by the Koochiching County beaver trapper in chapter three, this feature is actually noted only rarely in sasquatch reports.)

Bob went over to where it had been and saw its tracks in the snow. Its stride was short in the thick brush but lengthened in open places. The prints were five-toed, 14-16 inches long, and 8-10 inches wide.

Mckenzie Lake, the scene of "Bob's" sighting.

The fish it had dropped, a northern pike, was lying there, and Bob saw that its stomach area was eaten out, but most of the meat was still intact. There was a red and white fishing lure in the fish's mouth which he took out and kept. He figured the fish had probably broken free from someone's line, died, and floated to shore where the creature found it. He followed the tracks for a short distance but lost the trail when he ran out of snow.

Bob thought at first that it must have been some kind of ape. Then he remembered circuses coming through over the years which had displayed "wild men" and began to think he may have seen an escaped wild man. He had heard family members and others say that these wild men had always lived in the area. There was even a story about a hunter having shot and killed such a creature in the Buckboard Hills back in the 1920s and burying it deep in the forest because it looked so human that he feared being charged with murder.

Bob says in the years since his sighting, he has occasionally seen trees chewed on, which he feels may be the work of these creatures. Today he is fairly certain it was a sasquatch he saw, and he says it looked almost exactly like the one in the famous 1967 Roger Patterson film (although that creature was a female with black, not brown, hair.)

This type of creature has been described countless times over the years in widely separated areas across North America. With its humanlike feet, it could not be the species responsible for Ed Trimble's discoveries. Ed admits this and seems to believe that the two types may not interact or get along with each other very well.

I felt that Bob's account was very believable. He had an excellent memory for detail even after 31 years, and he was very specific in stating that he wanted no publicity from his story.

(Incidentally, the story of the creature being killed is, of course, impossible to verify after so many years, but even if it is true, the area is so large and wild that I wouldn't even begin to think about locating the body today.)

The next report belongs to a man Ed met one day at the Long Lake Campground, Daniel Tweten. The two got to talking, and eventually, this story came out. It happened in January of 1963 between the towns of Leonard and Shevlin, toward the northern end of Clearwater County.

Ed later conducted a taped interview with Tweten on April 24, 1992:

DAN TWEIEN: My name is Dan Iweten, 41 years old, native of northern Minnesota, spent probably half my life or better in Clearwater County. I'm a member of NRA, North

American Hunting Club, life member, I've hunted since I was about old enough to walk- trapping and studying wildlife, what have you.

Winter of 1963, got a lot of snow, we'd had some pretty severely cold weather, and my mother and I had went down to the woods to bring out more firewood.

Left the car and trailer on the side of the road and took hand sleighs, and went back into the tamaracks to take and get wood. We'd brought out... I don't know, three, maybe four trips, when I discovered some tracks off to the side of our trail. To the best of my recollection, the tracks were approximately a foot long, if I remember correctly were four-toed, with a- they were flat-foot, but there was like a lump or a pad under if I remember right would be the... outside edge of the foot near the heel. The tracks were approximately four feet apart. I called my mother over to look at the tracks. She got a little bit paranoid, said we better head out of the woods. The farther we went, the more she thought that the thing was after us, to where she had me about shaking in my boots. Tipped over the sleigh of wood, and she said to heck with the wood, just bring the sleigh, let's get out of here. We got out to the car and went home, and she instructed me as not to mention the incident to anybody 'cause nobody would believe us. And she kept me out of the woods for- oh, seven days, ten days, in that neighborhood.

I went back to the back side of our property- I imagine I was squirrel hunting- and I found tracks on the logging road that were approximately 14 to 16 inches long. I might be stretching it a little bit, I don't know. I believe they were four-toed also, and those tracks would've been- the stride would've been approximately five and a half feet, in that neighborhood, 'cause I would take two steps between each step that the animal took. Maybe not nice to take and call it an animal. Might be human (laughs).

ED TRIMBLE: Humanoid.

DAN: There. Humanoid. I started following the tracks. This was late in the afternoon, and I'm guessing the time of year at that point... some time in January. At this particular point, we were having some very mild warm weather after a severe cold. I followed the tracks for approximately two, two and a half miles, maybe a little bit farther. They were about as straight a line as if you'd fire a rifle. There was one fence at the end of the property on our land, was a sheep netting, and then there were two, three barbed wires on top that were tight, 'cause I remember walking back and forth alongside the fence to find a place where I could get over the fence, and Bigfoot had, to all appearances, just stepped over, never broke stride. Just kept steady walking. Didn't seem like anything moved it unless there was a tree directly in its path. The country was swampy to rolling hills. There was no indication that he had stopped at any point. It appeared to have just had its mind made up where it was going and wasn't wasting any time getting there.

(Note: Crossing a high fence in one step without breaking stride, as described here, is a feat that comes up every now and then in sasquatch reports across North America and is impossible for most human beings.)

Towards dark, I came up a hill that had a lot of pine on top. The snow was sparse to non-existent on the top of the hill, and I lost the tracks. And also, it was getting dark, and I ended up not knowing for sure exactly where I was at, and I ended up spending the night under one of the big pines there on top of the hill 'til morning light and then went on home- to a very upset mother. 'Cause I would've been 13 at the time, and she was slightly worried about her little boy out in the woods. That about wraps up my encounter with the tracks.

ED: She had told you not to follow those tracks.

DAN: Yes. The first time, when we first found them in the woods, she would not let me go back down there. She- I don't know if she has ever seen anything of [that] nature before or what, but she was awful, awful scared. And she told me to stay the heck out of the tamaracks down there.

ED: You couldn't even go back and get the wood that had been cut.

DAN: No... Later, closer to spring, we went back and got more wood, but there was a period of several weeks... that she wouldn't let me go anywhere near the tamaracks.

...It's been a fascination for me, anything with Bigfoot or that. I've never really done any studying or anything on it, but if I hear anything, it's something that interests me. It's a puzzle in my mind, a big question mark.

Tweten also said that in 1972 or 1973, he had seen similar tracks in the Black Hills of South Dakota in some soft soil by a stream at an abandoned gold mining camp, but he couldn't be sure about them (see chapter twenty-two).

The next Clearwater County story came from 39-year-old David Sunderland. He could not remember the exact date of his experience, but it had occurred in mid-October, sometime between 1968 to 1970.

The location was within a few miles of Ed Trimble's home, and the story told of the sighting of a manlike figure of truly immense size.

I conducted a taped interview with David, with Ed sitting in as well. Here is a partial transcript:

DAVID SUNDERLAND: My brothers and I were hunting ducks over there on Hawk Lake... They were around behind the lake, and I had pulled up at the car there and

I was waiting for them to come out, and I was looking across the fields. I don't

know why I was looking over that way... I seen something walking on the fields over there. And ah, it looked so tall and so big and covered so much ground, and there was a tree out in the middle of the field, a pretty good-sized tree, and when it walked past that tree, it was so high up on that tree, and that's why I didn't think it was a human 'cause it was so dog-gone tall. You know, it was way up on the tree when it passed it. But it was- you know, it was quite a ways off, but it looked awful big, and it covered that field real fast, just walking. I watched it for a while, and finally, it disappeared in the woods... To me, it looked weird, you know, but after it was gone, it was over with, so I didn't- I never said nothing about it. I didn't realize what it could be, but- I mean, it didn't look like no way it could be a human 'cause it was too big.

MYSELF: About how tall did you think it was?

DAVID: Oh, there was no way I could tell. It was just bigger than what it would be for that distance. The distance I was looking at it, I suppose it's gotta be at least (a quarter-mile), and it looked awful tall... A human walking that far away don't look very big, and this looked awful big and tall.

MYSELF: Did you go over to where it was and see if there was any sign?

DAVID: No, no. I never walked over there.

ED TRIMBLE: It wasn't a cultivated field.

DAVID: No... But um- I don't know. I just never gave it much thought after that. I just thought it was something I seen and didn't know what it was.

It just seemed weird. And it covered ground fast walking. Like it had a real long gait, it could cover ground real fast. It wasn't running, it was just walking. It covered that field fast walking.

ED: Swinging its arms?

DAVID: Yeah, I can remember arms swinging somewhat. The arms hung down, you know, so—

ED: Didn't look back.

DAVID: Nope.

MYSELF: Do you think it saw you?

DAVID: No, no. No, I was way over, sitting in the vehicle. I was looking for them guys, I wanted them to come out and see if they could see it too, you know, but they was just gone. (Laughs.) When you see it by yourself, you start to wonder, "What the hell did I see?" you know, if it was me or somebody else or am I crazy or what, so you- then you don't just- you just shrug it off.

MYSELF: What time of day was that at?

DAVID: Oh, I suppose in the afternoon... about 4:00.

MYSELF: Was it a pretty clear day, good weather?

DAVID: Yeah... Other than that, I don't know what else I can tell you about

that.

MYSELF: It was just you that saw it?

DAVID: Just me that saw it, yeah. No other witnesses. (Laughs.) It would've been nicer if there would've been another person with me, but—

MYSELF: Yeah. Was there a lot of woods beside that field?

DAVID: Well, yeah, it was walking into the woods. When I started seeing it, I suppose it was already- halfway across the field before I seen it... and then it didn't take long before it was in the woods on the other side.

ED: I suppose that tree is gone now.

DAVID: Bulldozed out. But ah, I remember that tree that stood out there all by itself, and when it walked by that tree, that's when it really bothered me, 'cause it was high up on the tree. It just- didn't look right.

MYSELF: But you couldn't tell how high?

DAVID: No, there was no way to judge the height.

MYSELF: Could you see what color it was?

DAVID: It was just a- there was no color to it at all. It was just a dark- I don't know, what would you say- brown or darkish color, you know. It wasn't- there was no whites on it or anything. It was just one solid dark color. I couldn't see no- like hair or anything on it from that distance. It was too far away.

MYSELF: But it seemed to have the same basic shape as a person?

DAVID: Yup. It did, yeah. Well, when I first saw it, that's what I thought, you know, it must be a hunter or somebody walking out there, but I couldn't figure out why they'd be out there hunting anyway because there's really no good woods there to hunt there. There ain't no ducks there to hunt unless they're out hunting partridge, but in that area, I didn't know who'd be out walking. And then when it got to that tree is when I realized that it was- you know, it was a lot bigger than a human being.

MYSELF: Did you tell anybody about it at the time?

DAVID: Never told anybody about it...

MYSELF: Well, if I ever write something about this, would you mind if I use your name?

DAVID: No, I don't care... it doesn't really matter if the other people that read it believe me or not. (Laughs.) It doesn't matter, I don't care. It wasn't- bragging what I seen, it's just something crazy I seen, you know.

Although David said on the tape that he could not judge the figure's height, off-tape, he recalled that it was half as tall as the tree and that the tree was about 20 feet tall. This raises the question of how something ten feet tall could be reported seen only once in such an area, but David had told no one but his family about it, so perhaps other witnesses could be equally tight-lipped. Not everyone wants to admit that they've seen a giant walking across their field.

Speaking of his family, you may recall that David's father, Stanley Sunderland, also sighted an unusual creature in 1980 near International Falls (see chapter three).

(It may be significant that Stanley also once had two 50-pound blocks of salt, placed out in the wild to attract deer into an area prior to hunting season, disappear without a trace from his land. No animal would have been able to make off with them; it would definitely take something with hands. Either human trespassers were responsible or something more mysterious.)

The incident in the next story to come my way had occurred on the property of Stanley's brother, who lives quite close to the scene of David's sighting, in the fall of either 1971 or 1972. The storyteller was Wayne Thompson, 39 years old when I interviewed him in 1991, who lives now down in the Twin Cities area but through good fortune happened to be around his old home when I was in Clearwater County.

The story of "Bob" from 1960 had included a terrible odor coming from the creature, and that feature turned up again in Wayne's account.

WAYNE THOMPSON: Where it happened was down on Jennings Sunderland's field... me and this friend of mine, Bill Rutherford, were grouse hunting... It was either like the first or second weekend of grouse season, 'cause all the leaves were on the trees. And ah, off the end of Jennings' field, going toward that lower Rice Lake area, there was this logging trail that went on the end of the field, ok? Bill and I, you know, were grouse hunting, so we walked off the end of this field down this logging trail, and we only got about- probably 50 to 75 yards into the woods or off the field on this trail, and- I'm not exactly sure when we started smelling this smell, it was kind of a skunky, pretty fairly strong skunky odor. But it wasn't a skunk- that much I could tell, but it was a skunky odor. And I think just kind of as we entered the woods, we started smelling this, and we walked to one side of the trail we were on- we heard the bushes rustling. And we stopped- neither one of us said a thing- we stopped, and looked, and ah, probably- there was some shorter- there was a lot of leaves, and it was real thick brush. But there was some taller brush, and we could see this brush wiggling, so we knew exactly where this, whatever-it-was was doing this, was right there. About 75 feet... was how far away the brush was wiggling, probably for 10 or 15 seconds, the brush just kind of rustled around there. And then we could hear—

MYSELF: Just in one spot?

WAYNE: Yeah. It was kind of just in one spot because there was a lot of- that's the only place we could see it rustling. But then- this was for about 10 or 15- I can't remember that for sure, how long, but it wasn't real long, then we could hear this, whatever it was, going down, moving away walking. It would've been a northwesterly direction. But we could hear it walking down through the woods. It wasn't running.

MYSELF: You could hear the footsteps?

WAYNE: Oh, yeah. And it sounded- it's something that- you know, it sounded- it was absolutely no deer, 'cause I've hunted a lot of deer, and I know what deer sound like going through the woods and it wasn't a deer. And it sounded just like a person, if it had been a person walking down through the woods is what it sounded like. You could hear each individual step. You know, just step, step, step, step, until I couldn't hear it no more. I've never forgotten about that, and I've always wondered what it was... but I have no idea.

MYSELF: Did you go over where it was and look for any sign or anything?

WAYNE: Yeah, I think we looked around there, but we- you know, like it was- with all the brush and all the leaves and stuff, I didn't find anything.

I believe we looked around there a little bit, but we were a little bit leery, (laughs), you know, 'cause all we had were shotguns- 7 1/2 shot... At the time, we didn't go after it, I know that. I don't remember for sure if we looked around- I think we did look around but we didn't really see nothing that I can remember. But we did not go after the direction that the footsteps went, I know that.

MYSELF: Did you have any idea at the time what it might've been?

WAYNE: No. Ah, I- the only- I don't remember thinking of it as being Bigfoot, but I thought, well, you know, maybe possibly a bear, but I have no idea. And I still don't know, but I remember that strong, strong skunky odor, and then the brush, the rustling right there.

It was an honest, straightforward report with no speculation in it. Wayne did not know what he and his friend had heard and smelled and he admitted it. He did now seem to think, though, after hearing of Ed Trimble's discoveries and of other peoples' stories, that it was possible he had encountered a sasquatch. Possible, but not definite.

Ed told me of a similar report made by a woman who worked as a librarian in Bagley. She had been picking berries in the Zerkel area (Ed did not recall the date) when, like Wayne, she suddenly smelled a foul or strong odor something like a wet dog and then heard something very large moving in the nearby brush. She did not see what caused the disturbance. Later she asked Ed what a bear smelled like.

I don't believe sasquatch ever entered her mind but she did not know what it could have been.

There was apparently a man writing a book at the time, a collection of local stories from the area, and he got wind of the woman's experience. He talked to her about it, believing she had met a bear, but she could not confirm that. As Ed put it, however, the bear did find its way into the book.

That kind of story is about as far from conclusive as you can get, but it's just enough to keep you looking for more. And sure enough, there is more. And then some.

The story of Gerald and Edna Wraa, old friends of Ed's, goes off on quite a tangent but does have a definite relation to the sasquatch phenomenon. Parts of it, however, are downright bizarre, and it is the kind of story that most sasquatch hunters like to stay clear of.

The Wraas live near the town of Leonard, the same area where some of the more conventional reports are from, and their experience took place from around 1970 to 1972. Again, Ed's tape recorder took down their account:

GERALD WRAA: Well, my name is Gerald Wraa. I live up in Clover Township, that's the northern part of Clearwater County, and we moved in here- my wife and I, we were married in about '47, I think it was, and we settled in this country, so we've been here for 40 years. I've worked in the woods all my life and trapped- I started when I was a young fella, seven, eight years old, I guess. Trapped over the years, different kinds of animals, and observed the woods, worked in the woods, so we get knowledge of it, sort of. What we see and understand.

And we have an experience here. Ed Trimble and his wife Nova is here this afternoon, and I'm going to tell them a little story about something that happened here- back about 20 years ago, I believe. We had a garden that was tilled up, and in the morning I went out there and I seen these strange tracks. They went into the garden and came out again, about- oh, kind of a semi-circle there. And the tracks were so different, I'd never seen them before. They were probably a foot long, as well as I can remember, had three toes on them about all the same length, and they were spread about the same way. And the foot went- the overall length of it was about 12 inches, and then the strange part about it was there was a heel there, and the impression into the ground was that it would be quite heavy. At first, I thought maybe it was a bird, then I got to thinking, well, there's no such thing around here that size. And so my wife looked at it, and she accused me of playing a trick on her. And then our pastor was over that morning, and he did the same thing. And we were really puzzled by it. And then a couple weeks later, we seen this same track again, only it had rained, and it was in the road. Quite deep prints in there, so you could tell that it was heavy.

And we had different people out looking at it- Gunder Swanson, he was an old trapper or a local lumberjack some 90 years old, and he'd never seen anything like it before. And different people heard about it, and they came out and looked, and nobody seemed to know. And the DNR- we phoned them, and we'd get no satisfaction, they didn't seem to know anything about it.

Then I guess relating to this was this strange thing that used to come through our yard at that same time. That happened several times that summer. It made a noise when it came through the yard, and then the odor from it was so terrible, the smell would come right in the house, and you could hardly stand it. And the next morning outside the house, there was no odor, so it seemed like it just appeared when- whatever was there. And this happened several times that summer- early spring and summer, I guess it was.

And then we also found a- my wife found a ball of fur out there... a rolled up ball of fur, and we didn't know where that came from. That was a mystery. So we just don't know.

EDNA WRAA: The occurrence was quite regularly that first year as I remember, the occurrence of the smell, and it was always during the night. And it was such a strong, putrid, penetrating smell- something different than anything I had ever experienced. I've lived- I was born and raised in this country, right here about a half a mile up the road I was born- and pretty much knowledgeable about different experiences and odors of animals, but this was different that I have never experienced before. It was such a penetrating smell, it just came through the house, and I remember at night it would come, that smell, and I'd cover my head up with the blankets and try to get away from it, but it- every place, you just couldn't get away from it. I remember even running down to the basement and thinking I could get away from it there, and it was just as strong there. And the strangest thing was that in the morning, it would be gone. And I never experienced any fear over it, it was just- it happened so regularly that first year that it got so I'd wake up, you know- the smell was so strong it would wake one up- and I'd say, "Oh no, not again. Not that horrible smell again." And it would leave a bitterness in the throat, almost. You could almost taste it, it was so harsh, so strong, so bitter. Something different. Another thing I'd been thinking about is we talked about that I never had any fear of whatever that type of animal- we related it to the tracks. We related that odor to what the tracks was and the noise to the tracks. But I never had any fear about it. It was just more of a dread of that horrible smell.

ED TRIMBLE: Well, let's describe the noise. How often did that occur?

EDNA: ...It would be here, and then it would be there, it would go so quick. Like- at first, we thought it was a bird, because it seemed like it went so fast, we thought it's a bird flying through the yard.

GERALD: But it wasn't a bird sound.

EDNA: It was, ah- screeching. Strange.

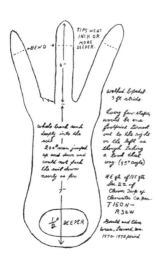

Drawing of the strange track seen by Gerald and Edna Wraa

GERALD: Yeah, kind of a screechy noise, or- "Eeeeee..." that was about the way it was, the way it sounded.

ED: How long did it last each time? A second or two?

GERALD: Probably a second... Yeah, it wouldn't be no more than that, I wouldn't think.

ED: And it was high pitched, and even.

GERALD: Right. Yup. Something we'd never heard before. Like we say, we're acquainted with things in the woods, and we hear things, and we automatically figured out it's something that's- you understand, when you're in the woods you hear something and you know right away without thinking or figuring it. But this is something we never heard before, something entirely different. Smell, noise, tracks- and at that time we also, at that period of time, we seen these, ah- UFO, we thought it was. We didn't- not for sure, but observing it, that's what it looked like. It was that same year. So we thought at the time that... it was maybe strange people (laughs). I don't know.

(The "UFO" Mr. Wraa mentions was a greenish-colored light that would fly quickly from place to place just above the treetops.)

EDNA: If I remember right, this went on, though, for a couple of years, maybe more... it seemed like it come around springtime and early summer... a couple years or so it visited us- visited us and got to know us and left us again (laughs).

GERALD (about the sounds): ...This was right out in front of our front yard there. Right in the yard, just 20 feet from the house.

EDNA: Yeah. That's where I found- I remember, one morning

after this putrid smell during the night... I was puzzled because there was no odor at all in

the yard the next day, and I went out looking around to see if I could find some

tracks or something to figure out what it was, and then I did find that ball of hair, some hair in the yard. And we had a black dog at that time... and if I remember right, the hair that I found was either a grayish-white or a brownish-white. It was a light color, anyway... And it didn't seem to bother the dog, that's another strange thing. The dog didn't bark at it, it didn't seem to alarm the dog

any.

GERALD: Everything else bothers him. Used to. He was a good watchdog...

And the boys were- Joel, our second boy- he was trying to tape-record some of the noise when it went through...

EDNA: It went so fast that by the time he got the recorder on, it was gone.

ED: ...You mentioned this heavy man comparing how far he sunk into these

tracks... How much did he weigh?

EDNA: 240, I think they said, or 230... It was a heavy creature.

(A young man of this weight had jumped up and down trying to match the depth of the three-toed tracks and didn't come close.)

GERALD: The first thing when I seen it, I thought, well, it would be a bird track, you know, but then it's too heavy for that. And the way it walked, it would take about a three-foot step, and then once in a while, one of the foots

would turn in... And then it would straighten out, take two, three steps, and

then it would turn in again...

ED: First one way and then the other way.

GERALD: Yeah.

ED: Which could be when it wanted to take a look to its left or to its right.

GERALD: That could be... And then I was going to mention too that at that

same time we had a salt block that we generally put out every year for deer... a big salt block. And this disappeared. And I told my wife I just put it out, and it was gone, and I thought at the time maybe some hunter had come through there or walked through and picked it up and took it some place else, but it's such a wild area- it's north of our place, along the lake, and I don't know who'd ever walk through there, so that was kind of a different thing, too. And that hasn't happened since. We've put out blocks, put out one this year even, and it's still there.

ED: Well, one of our neighbors (Stanley Sunderland) reported years ago having two salt blocks totally disappear, they never found them, and this is an area where they had planned to hunt deer later on, and it was an area where Bigfoot had been sighted.

GERALD: Well, there's some relation there, all right, to that.

Also, at that time, an incident not mentioned on the tape involved the Wraas finding some sharpened stakes about the size of broomsticks stuck in the ground in a random pattern in a grassy or brushy area near their home- not a bizarre thing but something they never could explain.

The sketch in this book of one of the footprints described by the Wraas shows their high strangeness. They do not even exactly match other three-toed tracks attributed to the sasquatch in other areas. Add to that the flying lights so suggestive of a UFO-type presence, and we are left here with a story that can only leave us guessing.

Still, another recording made by Ed tells the story of Mr. and Mrs. Terry Johnson, who had two odd experiences nine years apart at their home on Falk Lake near Clearbrook. We are back now to a much more down to earth account:

TERRY JOHNSON: My name's Terry Johnson. I moved here in 1980, fall of 1980, to a place seven miles east of Clearbrook on the west side of Falk Lake. In the process of laying the foundation for part of my home in mid-June, early July, I was startled to hear a little bit of a noise coming through the brush along the edge of the lake, which is about 150 feet from our work site. Along with the crashing through the brush, we could also hear a little bit of a heavy breathing noise that just sounded like a large animal. Didn't really know or understand what the noise was that we were hearing, but heard that it was getting closer and closer and louder. And ah—assumed that it probably was a bear just crashing along through the brush. Ah- evidently, the bears don't make that kind of a sound, but I didn't know that then. Also accompanying this sound that we heard was a rather strong, offensive odor- the best equivalent I could say would be about the same thing as the lion house at the zoo. Very, very strong offensive odor. And ah, never did proceed- my wife was interested in going to look to see what it was, but I suggested that she just better not stick her nose in where it didn't belong and just stay put. The whole incident lasted maybe three to four minutes, and then quietly, whatever it was, just disappeared. Have no idea what it was.

I guess the other incident that comes to mind was seven or eight years later, in 1989, I would say (actually nine years later). This was, ah- late or mid-evening, nine-thirty, ten o'clock- and a good distance away, I heard three- what sounded like three coon hounds running an animal. Very very excited, running an animal, and as it proceeded the- I could hear the brush breaking ahead of the hounds, and it got louder and louder to the point where I could hear what had to be two and a half to three-inch saplings getting busted over. One after the other, many many many saplings. For a period of probably five minutes, these hounds chased whatever this was, breaking down very, very large saplings. Again, I didn't see anything at all. This was pitch black, dark, and at least half a mile away from me, across a field going through fairly heavy swampy woods. That's about it. Any questions, Ed?

ED TRIMBLE: Well, on the first one, how great a distance did it travel in these approximately four minutes? How many yards would you say? ...Couple hundred yards?

TERRY: No, no. Not that far. It was quite a bit closer than that when we first heard it. I would say- a hundred yards. A hundred yards was the distance, but I'm just doing that from the sound, where I would place the sound. Probably a hundred yards.

ED: The closest it came to where you people were was perhaps-50 feet?

TERRY: No. No, more. It would be more like 150 feet...(Later, about the smell) ...It was amazing that it would be that strong- and to think that it would be that far away and yet be that strong. But maybe the wind was just right coming up off the lake or something. But that's about it, and never did pursue going to look at it or anything. I wish I had many times afterwards, but I figured for sure it would be a bear, 'cause I thought I had heard that bears are pretty stinky, but evidently not, so— (laughs).

ED: Not in my estimation. I've had some experience with them. I haven't heard anyone else say that, either... They eat some terrible stuff, but somehow they don't seem to get much of it on them or get rid of it somehow.

TERRY: Well, I was laboring under a misconception, then. But it was still pretty interesting to me. I thought you know- I should really have gone and looked to see what it was, but I was busy with my cement work.

ED: You might have been able to find tracks there and see how long the stride was and whether it looked like four feet or just two, but- I can think of a lot of things I should've done on those first track sightings that I saw (laughs), and I didn't do them either. It's as though I was stupefied.

TERRY: Yeah, if we had the chance to do it over again—

ED: You might, someday.

TERRY: Yeah, well, I'll keep an eye out for him, that's for sure. Whatever it was.

Between Johnson's two incidents on the time scale, there were three others that Ed became aware of. As a researcher, I have to envy the way these reports just keep falling into his lap.

The first took place somewhere from 1980 to 1983, to the best of his personal recollection. He described it in a letter:

"Several years ago, there was a lost person search in the general area of Alida and Becida. It included a team using trained hounds from Missouri, large search teams both local and from a distance, planes, and choppers, some with sensors. This search, intensive and extensive as it was, failed. A hunter, later on, found the remains- and not far from the home this person had strayed from.

"One report the authorities checked on during that time was of a sighting of a person standing at the edge of the woods near the Mississippi River. Saturday evening, I, at last, had a chance to question the man who had reported it. He said that he could not confirm that he really saw a human or a humanlike creature because it was at quite a distance (across 40 acres, he said), and the light wasn't good and that he supposed that his eyes could have played tricks on him.

"He couldn't say that it walked either sidewise to his position or retreating into the woods and did not report movement of any kind.

"Now, this man would not be a publicity seeker- far from it. Whatever he saw made a strong enough impression on him to cause him to report it in spite of

the fact that doing so would put his name in the records of that search effort - and in the papers that were covering the effort, too. This man is a native of the area, a farmer and woodsman, family man, school bus driver for many years, and I've never heard his name mentioned in connection with anything but just plain, honest, everyday affairs. I'm not going to press him further concerning this, but my feeling is that he had to be pretty sure that he saw something either human or resembling human in form to cause him to 'have the publicity' of reporting it."

(The missing person in this case, incidentally, was an elderly woman who had wandered away from her home.)

In another letter, Ed told the following story:

"Eighty-three year experienced, Mr. Alf J. Berg of Clearbrook, MN has hunted, trapped, fished, and traveled the wilderness areas extensively. He also has the 'Best Checkers Player Around' reputation, which is the reason I found him, for I can't improve my game by playing pushovers!

"About ten years ago (would be 1984), Alf was driving along in a westerly direction about three miles south of town and getting near the Lindberg Lake area, which is in humpy-bumpy, hardwood, and brush surroundings. The lake is in a game reserve, and there are numerous beaver ponds and sloughs nearby but also some good farms with rich soil and very few field stones. It was a fair and pleasant midsummer day.

"Suddenly, at a distance of only about 50 yards, Alf saw what some of his Indian friends had long ago told him existed in the area. He says that it must have seen his car before he saw it, and he thinks someone must have been in the woods and flushed it out. It was six or seven foot tall, he estimates, and most vividly, he recalls that it had long dark gray hair on its neck and shoulders. 'Very similar,' he said when I showed Stanley Sunderland's sketch to him (see chapter three). It was running through the short growth on farmer John Olson's meadow. Soon it was into the brush, but he could get glimpses of it now and then before it hit the woods. He thinks that he saw it for a total of less than a minute.

"He doesn't recall a pointy head in particular but seemed most impressed with how that long dark gray hair flowed out behind as it ran.

"'Fourteen inches long?' I asked.

"'Oh, yes,' he answered. 'Easily.'

"I feel honored that I am the first person to whom he's told this account."

Next, in discussing his track finds with some people, Ed knew they had commented, "Oh, that must be what our niece saw."

The niece was a part-Indian woman, initials L.L., whose experience had taken place in about 1987. She was said to have been driving in the Twin Lakes area near Nay Tah Waush, about 12 miles southwest of Zerkel in neighboring Mahnomen County, and to have seen a sasquatch running on or near the road ahead of her car. In looking at the speedometer, she saw that she was going 30 miles per hour but was not gaining on the sasquatch.

I would like to comment for a moment on the business of creatures being seen with extremely long head-neck-shoulder hair, as reported by Stanley Sunderland and Alf Berg. This is not a commonly reported feature by any means. Similarly, Ed had discovered extremely uncommon footprints. Could it be that these long-hairs are the ones responsible for the odd roundish tracks?

I was once told of another such creature being seen by some hunters in a wild region of Ohio, who had heard stories of a very strange bear being seen in the area. They thought they had spotted the animal and were watching it from some distance away in a swampy area but were surprised to see it throw its head back suddenly and send long wet hair flying around to slap against its back. They then realized it was no bear.

Various other stories from different locations have mentioned such long hair, to a degree where it just may indicate a specific type of creature. Only time will tell.

The next known experience would be that of Kim Fultz in early 1990, which was mentioned in the *Farmers Independent* article (see chapter 12). This would have been the first known appearance of the oddball roundish tracks seen later by Ed. The value of Kim's report is in how it corroborates Ed's finds, nearly a year in advance.

There was another track find at about the same time as Ed's March 1991 experience, but it was not learned of until some time later. It did not involve the same type of footprints, however, but much bigger ones. The man's story, again from Ed's tape recorder, goes like this:

MIKE POWERS: My name is Mike Powers, and my age is 44... and I'm gonna talk about my sighting of, ah- Bigfoot prints. The location of my sighting was the southeast corner of the northwest quarter of section 13 of Rice Township... near Mud lake (just a few miles from Ed's home). This sighting took place on or about the third week of March 1991. It was a nice sunny day, beautiful day. We had just bought land across from Long Lake, near Mud Lake, in November, and when we bought it, it already had the wood contract sold off of it, so I was up checking on this particular day the loggers, and I thought that being that it was such a beautiful day and the sun was shining that I would walk back to Mud Lake. And as I was walking back to Mud

Lake, after I passed the gate that separates my land from Richard Swanson's land, and I think that would be about four or five hundred feet into his little cabin which is on Mud Lake, as I was walking this road I came across some tracks that startled me I guess, to say the least. They were huge, human-type tracks that were coming from the south, going towards the north, right in the middle of this kind of a road, which is really more or less a trail. There was one huge, very clearly defined humanoid-type footprint that was- I would judge it to be 18 inches or longer- and I remember I looked at it, and I looked back into the south, and I could see where these prints had come for a couple prints back, and I looked to the north, and I could see a print or two going, and I don't know what I was thinking about that day, but apparently I- I don't know if I couldn't believe or didn't believe what it was- I thought it was a prank. That somebody must be playing a joke on somebody. And I walked on, and I went to the lake. I walked back and looked at them again and wasn't too overly concerned about them. In fact, I think I told my wife- maybe not at the time- but it was I would say maybe a week to ten days later, I happened to be over at the neighbors that are directly across from us on Long Lake and talking to them, and they were telling me about people in the area, and they happened to mention that Ed Trimble had seen some sort of Bigfootish-type tracks over by his place and I asked where his place was, and they told me and this whole thing came back to me. I said, jeez, you know, I seen something probably very similar to that over by Mud Lake. And I told them that, you know, maybe I had seen something like that too, that I wasn't sure what I had seen, but it was certainly the biggest footprint that I'd ever seen made by anything. And it wasn't until here now just this week when I talked to Ed, but he told me that his footprints were different, but this was definitely some sort of humanoid footprint and very, very large, as I said, and I don't know what I saw- you know, what it is- I didn't smell anything or see anything other than this- especially the- the others were blurred out, but the one that was in the middle of the road was just very distinct. And after I had been to the Simonsons, I hurried back up there to take a look again, but it was in the spring, and most of the snow had melted out, and there was nothing to be seen after I had come back.

ED TRIMBLE: Definitely a biped.

MIKE: Well, it must be. It was a humanoid-type footprint, but it was too big to be any humans, that I would say, especially at that time of year walking around without any shoes on. It would have been awfully cold.

ED: How long was the stride?

MIKE: I don't know, the stride I'd have to guess. It was probably twice that of a normal man, just taking a rough guess because I didn't examine the footprints very well on either side of the road, I just mainly looked at that big clear one that was right in the middle of the road.

ED: How did it affect you?

The trail between Long Lake and Mud Lake, where Mike Powers saw giant manlike footprints in March, 1991.

MIKE: Well, at the time I thought it was somebody playing a prank on somebody, and more or less that's what I thought until I had talked to the Simonsons, and then after that wished that I would've gone and got somebody, got a cast of it, shown it at least to one other person so that there could be some verification of what I saw there that day.

ED: You have been a hunter most of your life.

MIKE: Oh, yes. I've hunted a lot, you know. This wasn't a bear track, and this was nothing that you'd normally see in the woods that big is all I can say.

ED: Do you think that if someone saw a creature like that when he was hunting that he should shoot it?

MIKE: No, I don't think so. I don't think that anybody has, you know- just because we don't know what they are, I don't think anybody has the right to shoot them. Not even, you know, to catch a specimen or whatever. That's the way I feel.

ED: Well, there are some that say in some parts of the North American continent that they're numerous enough that some should be shot for scientific purposes.

MIKE: Well, I guess I have a different philosophy of life. I have a live and let live philosophy, and as far as I can tell, they've never hurt anybody unless

perhaps they were attacked or something, and- I don't know, that wouldn't be what I would do.

Then there was a report that caused me some confusion when it first came to me. It again involved "Bob," the 1960 witness.

There was at one time a "Bigfoot Hotline" sponsored by the California Bigfoot Organization, which Tim Olson had a hand in setting up. (Tim still takes calls on his own, but the CBFO has more or less disbanded now.) In the April 1991 issue of a newsletter called *The Bigfoot Co-Op,* there appeared a list of some reports phoned into the hotline during March, and one of them read:

"3/30/91- Bagley, MN- 'Tracks have always been here.' Saw prints in Nov. 1960 by McKenzie Lake. Saw creature sitting on a log eating a fish. Creature ran into forest. 1990- son was herding cattle and saw one. It stopped to pet dog, which cringed and ran away. So did the creature."

It was obviously "Bob" who had called, although he'd told me that the month of his sighting had been October, not November. Ed knew of the hotline and had spread the word about it somewhat in case others in his area wanted to report anything. When I had talked to "Bob," however, he had made no mention at all of his son having had a sighting the previous year. Besides that, a sasquatch petting a dog sounds completely ridiculous.

I inquired of Ed if he knew anything about this. In a letter, he responded:

"Yes, (Bob) must have tried the hotline. Can't tell if he's just having fun or if he is in favor of the search and trying to help... They run cattle way up in the north end of this county, and that is more of a herding situation, I think, and that's probably where the incident is supposed to have been."

So here we may have a second instance in which two people from the same family have had separate creature sightings. I suppose that if the sasquatch just reached out toward the dog for whatever reason, it might look like it was trying to pet it, but who knows? This is a report I should not conclude on unless I learn more about it.

Finally, there is a very vague report that happened to come my way through my brother-in-law. He heard from a man he occasionally works with about an old hermit-type fellow who lives near Shevlin, keeps a tame deer in his barn, is fond of whiskey and claims to see sasquatches around his home fairly often.

Alcohol is an easy explanation often used by skeptics, of course, but actually, it is <u>not</u> a hallucinogenic drug. Rather, it is a depressant that dulls the senses, and while it can sometimes make people see things depending on their state of mind if one is that intoxicated, it is more common for him not to remember what he really did see after he sobers up. Regardless of that, however, this is far too vague to conclude on.

15

NERVOUS ENCOUNTERS

B etween June 15-16, 1991, I had some spare time and decided to return once again to Clearwater County, but this time I told no one I was coming and did not plan to visit anyone. Talking to Ed and all the others was interesting, but it did tend to take away from the time spent out in the woods in actual searching for the sasquatch. I now intended to camp overnight in the Buckboard Hills and see if anything turned up there.

The forest was quiet, peaceful, and very rugged with its rolling up and down terrain. I saw only three or four other vehicles traversing the rough gravel roads in the two days I was there. At all other times, the solitude was absolute.

Ed had taken me through part of this wild area before. Now, while driving down a road he had not previously taken me down, I was wondering where I should pitch my tent for the night. My question was answered when I suddenly came across a sign reading "Arrow Point Campground- White Earth State Forest." Along the shore of medium-sized Rock Lake, about half a dozen campsites lay spread out. They all had fire pits, a few had picnic tables, and a single outhouse sat almost hidden in the thick woods. Other than that, there were no modern conveniences of any kind. It was a perfect spot, made all the better by the fact that no one else was using it at the time. After I set up my tent, I began to explore the area on foot.

I did not really expect to find anything. The usual result of a sasquatch hunt is to come up with absolutely nothing after hours of exhaustive searching (which has happened to me many times) and the few people in the field who claim to find footprints or to meet the creatures themselves practically every time they go out are almost never taken seriously. Thus, I almost feel guilty to report the fact that I did find something just a stone's throw away from my campsite.

One of my usual practices is to explore the edges of water sources for signs of the creatures since most all the animals of the forest have to come for a drink somewhere every day, so I decided to walk along the shore of the lake. It was hard going in some places, for the trees grew right down to the water's edge, forcing me to trudge through deep, sticky wet mud. I had been doing this for some time when, in the mud, I stumbled upon some curious-looking tracks.

There were two sizes: one 10" long and roughly 5" wide over its entire length, the other 8" long by 5" wide at the front end, 2 1/2" at the rear. The larger ones appeared to be somewhat bent lengthwise and did not show any toe impressions, while some of the smaller ones seemed to show just a hint of an indeterminate number of toes. They covered about ten feet of ground but were too randomly scattered to show a measurable stride, as if whatever made them had sometimes been stepping in the mud, sometimes in the water. They were several inches deep, with water in the bottoms of most.

The tracks were certainly not perfect, but in deep mud, they usually aren't. A person or heavy animal sinks in so deeply that in pulling out, the track is often distorted. Still, there was a definite conformity to the shape of these prints between each other, and it was obvious that two living beings of some kind had passed by.

Humans? It was not impossible, but the people most likely to be found at the lake's edge would be fishermen, and there were plenty of good fishing spots around that did not require slogging through mud and shoving overhanging branches out of your face.

Besides, the cumbersome boots required for such walking would not leave what looked anything like toe impressions.

As a little tease, another clue lay about 30 feet beyond the tracks. It was a dead turtle and quite a large one. It was crawling with insects, and no flesh remained, only bones and the bottom shell. The top shell was missing; something had pried it off. There was no way to tell whether the turtle had been killed on the spot or had washed ashore and been scavenged upon.

I poured plaster into the two best tracks (one of each size), still puzzling over them. By that time, evening was approaching.

Minnesota is notorious for its mosquitoes (some jokingly call them our state bird), and they closed in with a screaming vengeance with the setting of the hot sun. I tried to stay close to my campfire as much as possible to keep them away. I sat listening to the crazy song of our real state bird, loons, out on the lake, enjoying nature despite the bugs.

During the summertime in this state, the major part of sunset occurs after 9:00, and total darkness sometimes does not fall until 10:00 or so. At about 20 minutes to ten, I was sitting by the fire reading in the fading light when I heard a sound from the direction of the road. It sounded far away, and at first, I thought it was a person calling out. In a moment, I heard it again, closer this time, and now it sounded more like a dog barking.

Curious, I started walking toward the road. To my right, behind some trees, was the lake. To my left were a steep hill and the deep woods.

Apparently, the maker of the noise was also moving closer to me, and before long, I heard it clearly. Now I realized it was a sound I had never heard before, a raspy screeching that reminded me of a person running his fingernails along a metal screen, but several times louder. Whatever it was obviously had a powerful set of lungs. The sounds of crashing brush indicated it was something fairly large, and it was moving up the hill. Although it concealed itself in the shadowy forest, it did not seem shy about loudly announcing its presence to whoever cared to listen. Each of its calls lasted about a second, and they came sporadically, in no certain pattern.

Standing totally alone in the middle of the wilderness with the light all but gone and with god-knows-what approaching you with a sound that indicates a definite bad attitude is a feeling that can not be explained to someone who has not experienced it firsthand. Of course, I thought of a sasquatch. It was impossible not to. But there were other things it could have been as well, and any large animal can be dangerous if it gets angry enough. As quickly and cautiously as I could, I made my way back to camp while behind me, the unknown visitor continued its screeching. Then, after picking up a couple of important items, I summoned my courage and headed back toward it. In one hand, I held a camera, in the other a gun.

There are investigators who adamantly proclaim that a firearm has no place on a sasquatch hunt, people who believe the creatures are so rare and endangered that under no circumstances should one ever be shot. However, to those people, I would like to point out that Roger Patterson agreed with the no-kill policy but still did not object to being armed in the woods. In fact, his partner Bob Gimlin was pointing a rifle at the subject of Patterson's famous film even as it strode in front of the camera. In dealing with an animal as big as both of them, the men were taking no chances. This was my attitude as well. When going into an area believed to contain not only sasquatch but also numerous kinds of potentially dangerous predators, I think not carrying a precautionary weapon is ill-advised. This does not have to mean you are out to kill something.

The best example of the 10" track found at
Arrow Point.

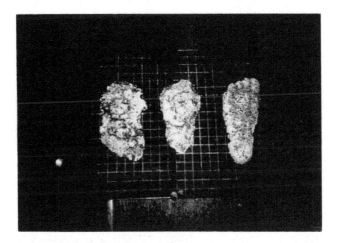

Casts of the Arrow Point tracks, one of each size, compared to a cast of a human track.

The scene of the author's June 15, 1991 track find
at Arrow Point Campground in the Buckboard Hills.
The dead turtle as it was found with its top shell

missing. A photo snapped in the dark in the hopes
of capturing on film the unknown animal arc Arrow
Point that made a strange screeching sound.

At the entrance to the campground, there is a trail that goes up the hill. I climbed it, homing in on the mysterious animal's vocalizations until I could hear the sounds very close by off to the left. I left the trail then and waded through the thick underbrush, finally reaching a high wall of brush that blocked my path. The darkness was just about total now, and I could not see how to get around it, but the source of the sounds was on the other side no more than 30 feet away.

My heart was pounding. I was asking myself, "Are you crazy?"

Even the mosquitos feasting on my blood seemed to be urging me to get away before the creature attacked, but I stayed put. I believe that a sasquatch hunter who pledges to actually go into the field and seek to confront the creature should be willing to put aside all fear and follow it into a pitch-black cave, up a tree, or even to jump on its back and tackle it if it is getting away before he's had a chance to get definite proof of its existence. I know that sounds completely off the wall, but this chase has gone on for too many years to allow any opportunity to slip away.

Of course, I couldn't say for sure what it was I was facing. It could have been something so ordinary that if a spotlight had suddenly revealed it, I would have laughed out loud in embarrassment, but whatever it was, it had stopped in one place where it continued its vocal display.

I noticed a small rock on the ground. Seeking to provoke the animal into making a move, I picked it up and tossed it over the bushes. The animal did react, but it did so by hurrying away in the opposite direction. Through the sound of crashing brush, I heard it make four or five of its calls, all strung together. Then there was silence.

I hastily found a way around the high foliage and saw that the thing had been in a small clearing, but there was no sign of it now.

I took a couple of quick photos in the dark in the hopes that it might show up somewhere in them (it didn't) and listened for its calls for a short time, then gave in at last to the fact that it had gotten away.

I went back to camp, still excited and nervous from my encounter. I had with me a copy of a recording made in 1972 in the California Sierras reported to be of sasquatch vocalizations, and I played it now at full volume, but even that provoked no further sounds from the woods. Getting to sleep that night then was not easy.

In the morning, I returned to the hilltop to look for tracks, but the leafy forest floor was not right for showing any. There was no sign of the nocturnal visitor to be found.

For most of the day, I searched various spots throughout the hills, scanning sandy and muddy areas for more tracks and walking down barely existent trails in the thick woods, but the excitement was over for this particular trip. Still, I had two plaster casts and a thrilling story to bring home with me.

Were the tracks in the mud, the mangled turtle, and the strange unseen noise maker in the night all related? I will probably never know.

During the weeks that followed, I got several opinions on what could have made the sounds. I wished I had managed to get a recording of them rather than have to rely on mere words to describe them (my sound equipment had been set up for broadcasting the California tape, not for recording), but I did the best I could.

A friend of mine who lived on a farm said, "Oh yeah, we have a bobcat in our woods sometimes at night that sounds like that."

A cat of some kind had occurred to me. Lynx and cougar seemed to be the best candidates, so I put the question to Ed Trimble. He responded in a letter:

"Your strange encounter at Arrow Point is a mystery to us, and we'd have to have a fuller description and then probably couldn't be sure of what it was. It doesn't seem that a Canada lynx would break any brush at all, they can thread their way through a fallen treetop with rotting and very brittle branches and twigs and not break a twig. Cougar that we've heard give a coarse, raspy, fairly loud call as they go along. Similar to a cat's meow but coarser and coming at spaced intervals- one neighbor said 'like a metronome.'"

And then there was the opinion of Samuel Sherry of the Ligonier, Pennsylvania area, who read my account of the incident in *The Sasquatch Report*. Sam has reportedly encountered the creatures himself a few times and is active in tracking them and attempting to prove their existence on Pennsylvania's Chestnut Ridge. He wrote:

"The sound you described was made by a Bigfoot as there is no animal that makes a sound like you described. The sound is made by blowing air through wet lips. The creature you heard had a friend nearby, he was sounding a warning signal. Bigfoots are capable of storing large supplies of air as they suck in air through the mouth. They do not breathe through their nose as they have no nose, just large nostril openings flattened lower against the face. No air sounds get through, they just smell with these openings."

Wow!

All good input, though Sam is usually considered pretty eccentric by most. I have never come to any firm conclusions on what I encountered in the Buckboard Hills. Yes, it could have been a sasquatch, but that is as much as I can say.

I can say more, though, about another incident involving strange sounds that occurred two years later.

Ed had been finding more strange tracks in his area (see the following chapter for a complete listing of all the track finds he has had to date). One of these turned up on June 17, 1993, and I was there to see it on the 21st. As it seemed, there were still creatures in the immediate area. I decided to camp out that night in the woods a little under a mile from Ed's property.

At around 10 p.m. (probably a little after), just after it had grown dark, I was having some supper by my campfire after a brief, light sprinkling of rain. You may notice that this was about the same time as the 1991 experience, and once again, I was startled to hear a sudden noise. It came from deeper woods perhaps a quarter-mile back toward Ed's home.

This sound was at once completely different and ten times more unnerving than what I'd heard at Arrow Point. Although far away, this call was so loud the woods practically shook with it. It is difficult to describe, but the closest comparison I can make is to some kind of Indian war cry with the voice of a police siren. There were short "WooPWooP" calls as well as long, drawn-out wails, all strung together in a wild, crazy outburst. I heard it twice, the first time lasting perhaps 20 seconds (by my approximation) and the second time, a few minutes later, a little farther away for not quite as long. It was extremely unsettling. Even when you are hoping for just such an event, nothing can prepare you for hearing something like that when you are all alone in a dark forest. I was thankful to have a weapon close at hand.

You may have read in other sasquatch literature about the semi-famous tape recordings made in Puyallup, Washington, back in the 1970s. They were made in conjunction with a number of creature sightings at the edge of the city. In his book "Sasquatch: The Apes Among Us," John Green describes the Puyallup sounds (which he personally heard) like this:

"The noise is not an 'eeeeeeee' scream, but more of a long 'whoo-OooOooOoo' or 'woopwoopwoop' at a high pitch and with immense volume... Heard from a distance it has been compared to the sound of a siren far off, but it is certainly not that."

Green and myself both making the comparison to a siren may be no coincidence. I've heard copies of some of the recordings made by the citizens of Puyallup, and I must say what I heard near Ed's home sounded extremely similar. The Puyallup sounds lacked most of the long-drawn-out calls (at least in the brief sample I've heard), but otherwise, they are a very close match.

So, while I remain unsure about the 1991 encounter, in June of 1993, I do believe I experienced the famous scream of the sasquatch.

Corroboration of this event came in a letter from Ed, dated August 12, 1993. He wrote:

"Ok, now I've heard what may be the same as you reported June 21st. First time was just before dark (around a week ago). It seemed pretty close... A loud cry lasting, I'd say, two or three secs, not high pitched, more like a man's voice- then this series of five whoops. 'Whoop' is the best word to describe it. (Low if compared to the usual coyote howl, not tenor or soprano but not low c either.)

"Last evening, shortly after eight, I heard first the cry- lasting four secs or more, I'd say- then in a minute or two another shorter one... After a few minutes, perhaps six or eight came the same cry followed by whoops. After the third or fourth whoop, one or more others joined in from the same location or slightly further west. There were no more cries, and [then] whoops, this time, may have lasted six secs or more.

"I've heard coyotes many times and at all seasons but never like this."

On April 2, 1994, Ed called and said he might have heard the mysterious calls again about a week previously. Four long cries- no whoops this time- each lasting seven or eight seconds and almost overlapping. This was far away to the southwest.

And finally, Ed learned about yet another incident of strange sounds being heard several years earlier in La Prarie Township, eight or ten miles to the northwest. A young couple described to him how they had heard a mysterious call that was apparently quite similar to what both he and I had heard, only more high pitched. Pitch, of course, is a very difficult thing to describe verbally after the fact unless you have the sound on tape, but this couple remarked that what they heard if compared to human sounds, would have been female. It consisted of a drawn-out call (about eight seconds) followed by the familiar whoops, only this time the descriptive word used was "roop."

Sasquatch, or aberrant coyotes? Hopefully, one day they will be seen at the same time they are heard.

16

MORE TRACK FINDS

People who report numerous sightings of the sasquatch or footprint findings are often looked upon with heavy skepticism. The creature is encountered by such a small percentage of the population, after all, that the odds are against any given person seeing a trace of one even once in a lifetime. When you think about it, though, this doesn't always have to be the way it works. If the creatures inhabit a certain area, any person who happens to live in that area has continual opportunities to see evidence of their presence, skeptics or no skeptics.

Ed Trimble has had more than just a couple of footprint finds, due partly to the fact that he goes out regularly to look for them and partly because he lives in such a wild area that the creatures evidently have no qualms about coming near his home.

Other evidence suggested that more than one species of creature can be found in the area, and the various tracks Ed has found support this idea as well.

In thinking back, Ed remembered what may have been his first track find way back in November of 1957. At the time, he was not yet really aware of anything like the sasquatch and so had no idea what he was looking at. As he tells it:

"I was back in that boggy wilderness near the tiny stream that feeds into Mud Lake near the north end. Had a .22 revolver and two five-gallon pails heavy with traps and gear, making cubby sets for bobcat. The first storm of winter was underway, it was snowing like crazy, light, fluffy stuff getting close to knee-deep.

"Here it was that I came upon a fresh set of tracks hard to accept and impossible to forget. It was impossible under those conditions to see details such as toes, etc., but the prints were big and the stride long. The critter wasn't going in the direction I wanted to go and, after seeing those tracks, I wanted even less to go that way. So I just followed, marveling, for a short ways and then resumed my cubby making.

"I had previously seen bear tracks in shallow, firmer snow, but I did not know - and I still do not know- if a black bear, going through deep snow, would adjust its gait so that the hindfoot would land where the front foot had. I think it's possible. Maybe someone knows for sure. If so, its trail would look as though made by a biped. If not so, then this is the first BF type sign I've seen— and it's absolutely unforgettable!"

Decades passed, and the next time Ed saw tracks he couldn't identify was the time of his now-famous discoveries in December 1990 and March 1991. But it didn't stop there.

The tracks of "Junior" may have appeared a third time on January 30, 1992, in the same pasture area as the previous ones in 1991, but they were mixed in with coyote tracks, and Ed could not be sure about them. Snow conditions were not the best.

The next find was a few months later, on April 12th, in the woods near the same pasture area. Ed wrote:

"We received two inches of snow, and there's lots of bare spots already. Was around the south yesterday PM... I came upon what looked to me to be the footprints

of the more usual type Sasquatch or Bigfoot- a small one- the prints only 8" long.

I took four pictures, two each of the clearest prints. The stride was but 16" going uphill, and the snow was so far gone in most places that I could not follow far."

A series of tracks of this type followed in 1993, but none as short as eight inches. The time span made us wonder- how fast does a young sasquatch grow?

January 27, 1993- Prints with three-foot stride, old and too melted out to show much detail.

April 7, 1993- A single print, the first found not in snow but in mud. Measured 11 1/4" long, 7" wide behind the toes, 4" near the heel. Toes not very distinct, 3/4" rock in middle of print.

Late May-Early June, 1993- Two finds in three weeks, both in uneven, rocky ground. One was of a single print; the other showed a partial second print with a stride of just over four feet. Length in both cases, approx. 11".

All of those were out in the woods along old logging trails, some distance from Ed's house. Then, however, the creature(s) started to come closer to home.

In mid-June, Ed was working on an earthen dike next to the pond near his house to prevent overflowing, bringing in wheel-barrow loads of rock and clay. On the morning of June 17th, he believes he narrowly missed out on seeing one of the creatures, frightening it away from beside the pond with the sound of his approach.

A fresh footprint was impressed into the clay of the dike when he got there, 11" long by $4k''$ wide at the ball and only $2k''$ at the heel. He wrote:

"...the toes do not show well enough to count (only two clearly showed)- the track is pressed in deep enough to indicate heft (approx. 2" deep where Ed's own tracks barely showed at all), but separate toe marks are smeared together as though creature was forcing itself ahead rapidly. There is no indication of claws."

The reason Ed thinks the creature was frightened is that it appeared to have made a sudden great leap. He later found a second print of the same dimensions 15' 5" beyond the first. It was hard to see as it was covered by swamp grass, as though the creature had jumped into concealment. Although shy, he thought it may have been curious about his work.

(It was when I came to see these tracks that I heard the strange cries in the woods- see the previous chapter.)

It was not impossible that a single creature was responsible for all of the 11" tracks (and with its little narrow heels, it is not likely to be a human being), but since Ed thinks he once heard more than one calling to each other the number of creatures in the area at that time remains a question. Whatever the case, though, a new exclamation mark was added to the story in mid-July- the return of Junior!

On the 14th of that month, I finally saw one of the oddball roundish tracks with its two large toe impressions firsthand, left in the same earthen dike as the previous manlike ones. In one place, it looked like just some toes had smeared the mud, but a few feet away was a whole print with a pressure ridge around it measuring only 7" x 6". If this was the same Junior, he hadn't grown any since his last appearance.

Also, across the pond, something had come and dug up a 10' x 6' area of frog and toad eggs out of the water. It looked like it had eaten the eggs and spit out the leftover grass and weeds.

Prints of a new size appeared on the dike in late July. On the 24th, Ed wrote:

"...new prints. One a left and one a right... Same size, 7 1/4" x 4" x 3", would be 38" stride if made at same time, but this is hard to accept. That is the only 'open' access to open, clear water... These prints not smeared, appeared to be straight forward travel, no leap. Could make out four toes in one."

These could have been Junior-type tracks, but they were too imperfect to be sure of.

One more small and rather unimpressive print appeared in early September of 1993 by a ditch Ed had dug to bring water down to the pond.

Just after this, a similar print showed up farther out in the woods, not good enough to photograph.

I myself found the final tracks of 1993 on October 7th while exploring the logging trails. They were in two spots at opposite ends of the same trail. Both finds were of single, partial prints, probably the familiar 11-incher (although Ed was rather skeptical of my finds). The night before, while camping out, I may have heard the strange cry again at a very long distance, but lasting only a couple of seconds. Unsure.

The next year brought still more discoveries.

On the morning of April 23rd, Ed found a print 9" long in wet ground. It appeared to be different from any previously seen and was on a steep upgrade. The pressure ridge around the print curled down before it dried.

Then on June 4th, I was with a friend, Kathy Keating of Moorhead, in the Buckboard Hills. In a newly logged area, on a side trail not far from Arrow Point Campground, I found a single print. It was 11" long, but not the same as the other prints of that length. The heel was wide, the toes even more so, with the greatest width being about 5 3/4". A slight pressure ridge surrounded the print, but the number of toes was unclear. It lay in the center of the sandy trail as if the creature had jumped across and touched the ground only once. Actually, it reminded me somewhat of certain tracks found in the eastern U.S.

Kathy was not all that impressed, but then she had only come along to do some fishing.

Ed's next find came in early September of 1994. By then, there were cattle pastured in the area where many of the tracks had been turning up, but he continued to explore the woods and trails. He wrote:

"The last time back, I saw what I feel sure is three more of what I call the third type tracks. None good enough to photograph- all three heading west and in the same little muddy place that the cattle hadn't spoiled... On the way back, something whistled off to my left. A short (less than second) low whistle such as is made by blowing across a shell casing. It sounded close. There was a cow standing in the timber and brush right about where I thought the whistle came from. Tara (Ed's dog) was off to the other side and was not excited about it. I'm sure that there wasn't any person doing it. I do not know of any bird or animal that whistles like that. It happened just once and seemed to come from about 60 yards away. It was in the afternoon of a pleasant day."

Finally, Ed found one last print in late April of 1995 not far from that one:

"...Did recently find another single footprint... 11 7/8" long, very narrow heel, forepart and toe area wide but indistinct as to details because of type soil and fact that some of last fall's leaves were over forepart of print, so blurred details such as number of toes."

I may have added one more page to the file on May 20, 1995, when Alan Weaver and I were exploring the logging trails near Arrow Point Campground. We found a possible sasquatch track at the edge of a deep trench gouged across one trail. A tiny stream flowed through at the bottom of the trench.

The track, which pointed toward the trench, was 14" long and hourglass-shaped. What appeared to be a couple of toe impressions were separated from the rest of the print by a pressure ridge. However, it was quite old, so it was uncertain, but just to keep us guessing, there was what looked like a deep heel mark about five feet down the nearly vertical slope.

Since there was only the one complete print, and since loggers had left a lot of boot tracks on the trail, the possibility of this being just a large boot track cannot be ruled out (that's what Alan thought it was).

There was one last observation that might be included here. In early August of 1994, Ed had written that he had heard from his friend Gerald Wraa (see his story in chapter 14) about bear trouble up in his part of the county. Large bears had been coming right into the Wraas' yard, and their tracks were everywhere. One track, in particular, found on a beaver dam, was of curious interest. It was 14" long

"Question is," Ed wrote, "do any black bear have a hindfoot that long? Personally, and offhand, I don't think so."

What should we make of all these little footprints? I certainly would not use them as hard evidence to convince a skeptic, for most of them have just not been all that impressive when viewed on an individual basis. Still, it almost seems as if curious youngsters have been roaming all about the countryside while the adults stayed hidden. The kind of giant tracks that spawned the name "Bigfoot" is not a total stranger to the area, though (see Mike Powers' 1991 report in chapter 14), so they're out there somewhere.

And Junior? Still around, apparently, but not in the company of the other type of creature. While they have walked the same ground at different times, their tracks have never actually been seen together.

Lest anyone should think that Ed Trimble goes totally crazy over every animal track bigger than a dog's that he sees, there is one more report that gives evidence of his ability to be objective.

On July 12, 1992, I received a phone call from Mr. Sonny Olson of rural Clearbrook. He said that that day his son had been disking in a field and had come across two sets of strange footprints which resembled the Trimble footprints pictured in my second book, "Creatures of the North." He doubted that they could be bear tracks as they looked to him to be bipedal. He added that a neighbor two miles away was missing two calves, with no tracks, fence damage, or any other traces of them.

Since Ed was close by, he was much better suited than I to check out this report, so I gave Mr. Olson his number.

Ed examined the tracks the next day and prepared the following report on them:

"Sonny, a logger, was in the woods, but his wife directed me to his brother's place, about 3/4 mile south, and I was shown the tracks.

"They were on a deeply plowed field, the soil of which was almost white and composed mostly of very fine sand. The plowing was done several weeks ago. The tracks weren't fresh and had had one big rain. It was plain that they weren't bipedal, but they did not seem to me to be typical bear tracks- a crippled one, I thought, perhaps. But too far gone to collect or photograph. The Olson brothers didn't know that a black bear's front feet have the largest toes on the outside, and these still showed far more clearly than the others- this, plus the fact that, in some places, the hindfoot came down in such a way as to make the footprint look like those we photographed here March 25, 1991. In many places, there was a 'heel' print behind the front footprint, just a short gap between. This was very clear, well-pressed in, perfectly round, and 2" or more in diameter. This puzzled me greatly, but I have now examined bear front feet and seen that it is a normal feature but that it doesn't show up in tracks that we see on most surfaces. (Later, Ed had the theory that the tracks may have been made by a male and female bear in the act of mating.)

"I did not take time to investigate the missing calf site two miles west or the farmer who had very mysterious losses of young cattle in previous years."

There are always false alarms.

On January 30, 1992, Ed Trimble found this line of footprints |with a three to four-foot stride. The prints on the right are Ed's own.

A few months later on April 12th, Ed found these small
8" manlike prints, evidently made by a young creature.
The tracks on the left are of Ed's dog.

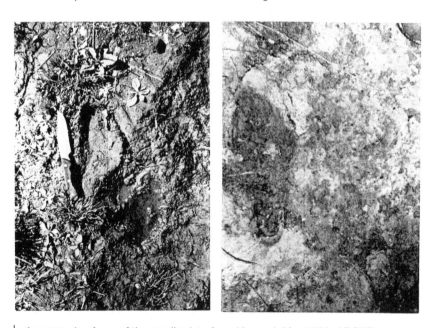

An example of one of the small prints found in mud, May 1993. ABOVE
RIGHT: 11" print on earthen dike next to Ed's pond, June 17, 1993.
This is where Ed feels he may have startled the creature and caused it
to leap for cover.

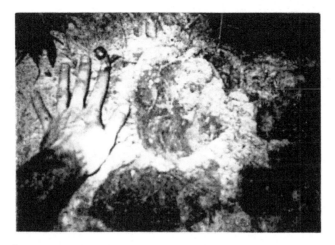

The track of "Junior" found in mud this time rather than
snow on July 14, 1993. Quite small and totally non-
typical, but very mysterious. A boot print lies along the
bottom of the picture.

An 11" track found by the author on June 4, 1994, in
the Buckboard Hills, compared to an 11 1/2" knife. This
is totally unlike other tracks of the same length found
by Ed Trimble.

17

NATURE'S TOOTHPICKS

The investigation in Clearwater County took a side trip for a while in 1991-92 when a lead picked up by Ed Trimble led us East- and into a most unexpected field of study.

In February of 1991, Ed wrote to me:

"I think I may have great news. Sent Mr. and Mrs. Homer Parson of Effie the four pages (his report about the tracks he found) and a note. These people are very well thought of in that locality... Homer was an expert timber wolf trapper. Heard right back today and letter urged me to call their son Clark this evening (Tuesday, Feb. 26, 1991). Just finished 15-minute talk with him... he has a place where he collects hair- reddish-brown and approx. 3" long, mostly right after snow goes off or around May 1st. Also sees indistinct tracks due to area they visit being grassy. Twice, he has had a glimpse of one. Bigfoot-type- said the one sitting on a log pile 'looked like a real big football player.' He has told some of his friends and insisted that they go with him to this spot and says it makes believers of them.

"Ok, so you mention that, in Kooch County, they have an attraction to 'the hum' of a high line. Are you sure that it's the hum? Do they visit highlines mounted on steel or just those on creosoted poles? Clark finds their teeth marks on the poles and says that they rub on them, leaving hair when they do! Says the hair is coarse. (Note: the Koochiching County powerline he mentions is mounted on steel support towers.)

"I suggested that they might rub a lot trying to rid themselves of ticks, but he thinks it's too early for tick time when they start. I'm not so sure, but he seems to think that they like the smell and perhaps the taste of it. We sometimes have ticks here before May 1st.

"Could it be that they've discovered that creosote is a repellent against ticks, lice, etc.? If so, is it still another sign of intelligence? Creosote has some medicinal properties, too- but please, don't let me get much of it on my hide!

"Clark thinks they eat the bark of white cedar. He dropped a bag of surplus garden produce, some sweet corn, rutabagas, etc. in a hole, rolled a big log over it, says they took it, went a ways with it but left it, couldn't tell if they ate any but thinks they may have sensed him coming to check. This would have had to be Aug. or Sept... Has not noticed any of their scats.

"He talked with man at Bell Museum of Natural History and was told that it was probably moose rubbing hair off on the pole. Offended. Says he knows moose tracks when he sees them.

"...I asked Clark if he'd heard the scream/bellow said to belong to B.F.

He said he hadn't, but a neighbor couple had. They've moved to Princeton, MN.

"...The place Clark Parson speaks of- he and friends have been there on ATVs (All Terrain Vehicles). Sounds as though his creatures are getting used to human activity."

At the time, I thought this Clark Parson must be either very lucky or one of the biggest storytellers in Minnesota, but obviously, his story had to be checked out. Unfortunately, due to other obligations, I was not able to do so until May of 1992. At that time, Ed and I took a trip to the area in question, which lies along the border of Koochiching and Itasca Counties between the towns of Wildwood and Effie, north of Bigfork.

The area looked much the same as most of the rest of northern

Minnesota- farms, logging roads, and mixed forest growth all over. Once we got there, we weren't sure exactly where to go but soon got directions from a few of the local people. That, and something more.

Ed is seldom shy about his interest in the "Bigfoot" subject, and he didn't mind describing to people our reason for being there. Some reacted with amusement, as can always be expected, but imagine our surprise when others freely volunteered their own accounts of strange goings-on in the area.

We met one old couple, Mr. and Mrs. V.P., who told us that they built a new house there in 1986 and that sometime shortly after that, Mrs. P had been out by the garage one day when she heard a high-pitched wavering cry that couldn't have been more than a mile away. She was apparently familiar with wildlife sounds and could not iden-tify the call. She didn't think it was a wolf, which she was well acquainted with as there were troublesome wolves in the area.

She also told of the experiences of a relative who lived just a short jump down the road. From this farm, an old trail winds its way back into deep woods. A couple of years after Mrs. P's experi-ence, the relative was about three miles down this trail when he found big scratches on a tree that reached nine feet above the ground. There was also golden or reddish hair snagged on the tree and a well-worn trail deeply impressed in the ground as if by some-thing heavy. (Actually, this sounds like the work of a climbing bear, but the odd hair color is of interest and may jibe with Clark Parson's report of reddish hair.) Ed and I were able to walk quite a distance down this trail and saw fresh bear tracks but nothing else of note.

When it came to locating Mr. Parson, we were disappointed to learn that he was away due to a family crisis; thus, we were not able to meet with him. We did meet his brother, Troy, however, who also lived in the area, and he was able to tell us a few extra pieces of information.

In the spring of about 1987, Troy said, he was on the Caldwell Forest Road near his home and stopped by a bridge to look for old bottles, which he collects. Just off the road, he found some large manlike footprints, four or five inches longer than a human's and fairly deep. He was able to take us there and show us the exact spot.

He thought it was at about that same time that his brother Clark came up with his own discoveries, which we already knew something about. Clark had taken him down the Cutfoot Forest Road, not far away, to show him another strange sign. Along this rough-cut road, there had once been a plant that treated logs with creosote and made them into power poles, with the workers living on site. The place was deserted now and in ruins, looking like some old rustic encampment. It was by these ruins that Clark showed his brother where branches had been broken off of some balsam trees, and there was just a single large manlike track on the ground. Clark thought the creature may have been swinging through the trees to avoid leaving tracks and had just briefly touched the ground by accident.

(Troy's son told us that his uncle Clark had photos of the big tracks he had seen, but we have not seen these.)

Not having Clark himself there to elaborate, we wondered if the site of the old treatment plant was where the poles were that supposedly showed signs of having been chewed and rubbed against by the creatures. Without too much effort, Ed and I found the site and were rewarded. There were no tall power poles, but several shorter ones were standing in various places, and many of them had definitely been laid into by some large animal.

There were a lot of wood fragments torn from the poles, some tiny and some up to two feet long, lying on the ground. Now, it's a well-established fact that the black bear will mark his territory by raking his sharp claws along tree trunks, and they are known to do this on man-made poles as well. But these poles were not clawed. They were bitten.

At various heights on the poles, some above our heads and some near the ground, the wood was gouged with horizontal and diagonal (but never vertical) teeth marks, two 1/4"-wide slashes that consistently measured 3 1/2" apart. It was exactly what one would expect from something with long eye teeth set in a wide jaw turning its head sideways and gnawing on the tar-stained wood.

Since that time, Ed has uncovered recorded instances of bears actually chewing as well as scratching on trees, but it seems to be a rather uncommon trait.

Added to this, it so happens that the eye teeth or "tusks" or even very large black bears measure only around 2 1/2" apart, so we are faced with an interesting puzzle here. Whatever our pole chewer was, its mouth was bigger than a black bear's.

A bigger species of bear? Needless to say, there are no grizzlies or polar bears in Minnesota, except in zoos.

But Clark Parson had seemed to be describing another place when he'd told Ed about his evidence. He'd spoken of tall highline poles, not these shorter ones we were looking at. Thus we made further inquiries and soon found that an old, inoperative highline led from the road back to some abandoned farm buildings near Troy Parson's home. We didn't get to this spot until after dark, and by the glow of flashlights, we made an eerie discovery.

Not just on a few, but on nearly every single pole in this line, we saw the exact same bite marks. Seeing them once was interesting; seeing them twice and in the dark was spooky. However, this damage was quite a bit older since there were no chips and fragments on the ground, even where large pieces had been torn from the poles. Whatever was responsible had gone at it so fiercely that a few poles were actually in danger of falling over.

Ed and I camped out at this spot, hoping to see or hear something during the night, but as is usually the case, nothing happened.

After this trip, Ed became interested in checking similar poles around his area in Clearwater County to see if the resident creatures were leaving their mark as well. To his surprise, not only did he find poles that were damaged by some kind of large animals, but it was happening currently. He started to visit the poles regularly and would sometimes find new markings. But this was different from what we had seen in the Wildwood region. It looked much more typical of bears, and Ed and I wanted to find out if the culprit was bear or Sasquatch (or indeed both, for why couldn't it be?).

Luckily there was a way to find out. A number of times, Ed found hair snagged on the poles. Tim Olson, out in California, arranged to have the hairs analyzed by Dr. Steven Busack in Oregon, who offers us his services in that regard in exchange for a subscription to our newsletter. I sent Dr. Busack four samples from different times. One that I was particularly curious about was tinged with red, an unusual shade for a bear.

The results of the testing, however, were disappointing. All four hair samples came from Ursus Americanus, the black bear. One of them was obviously in what is known as a cinnamon phase, hence the reddish tinge.

We had expected this result for at least some of the samples, wondering if the bear and the sasquatch might both have reason to put their marks on the poles, but it didn't go our way this time.

Still, I do not believe it was "just" bears that chewed the poles in the Wildwood area. The question arises: why would the sasquatch do this?

Some may theorize about a strange attraction to powerlines. The events described by DNR agent Harvey Cole in Koochiching County's bog country involved a powerline, and so did those in Vergas Trails. There was also one near the scenes of the New York Mills reports. (See chapters three, four, and five.) I've heard of cases in other states wherein sightings or track finds occurred along powerlines. Most of these involved steel support towers, however, not wooden poles, and besides that, the poles Ed and I found were supporting a deadline.

It could be a territorial marker. "Bob," the 1960 McKenzie Lake witness (see chapter 14) commented that he had sometimes seen trees in the woods chewed on and thought the sasquatch might be responsible, but he gave no reason for this belief.

Ed feels the most likely reason has something to do with the creosote, the tar coating the poles. It gives the wood a strong, distinct odor, the same odor you smell when crossing a railroad. The creatures may be attracted to that odor or even to the taste of the creosote, or as Ed has suggested, they may find that it helps keep insects away.

Whatever the case, this small phenomenon does not seem to be widespread. I am not aware of it having been reported anywhere else, but if anyone has, I would like very much to hear from them.

Ed Trimble examines damage to one of the poles along the Cutfoot Forest Road between Wildwood and Effie.

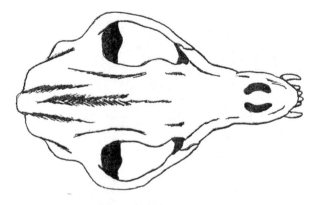

Top view of a black bear's skull showing the spacing of the eye teeth. Could the teeth marks on the wooden poles between Wildwood and Effie (shown close up in the photo below) have been the work of a bear?

Consider these figures: This diagram shows that the length of a black bear's skull is approximately 7 3/4 times the distance between the eye teeth. If those teeth were 3 1/2" apart, as were the marks on the poles, the bear's skull would be over 27" long. From this, we can figure that the animal would probably be around nine feet long and could stand over 12 feet tall on its hind legs.

And I challenge anyone to find a black bear that big in Minnesota or anywhere else.

18

RECOLLECTIONS

I t's hard enough to prove that one species of sasquatch walks the land, let alone two, but that's just the problem we have in Clearwater County. Both types are clearly present in the same area at the same time, a situation that makes for a great deal of speculation.

In all the areas across the country where more than one type of creature has been reported (and there are a few such places), at no time has it seemed that the different types mix with each other. They are not seen together, nor are their tracks found anywhere near each other. Even if they stayed apart, it seems that someone, somewhere, sometime would have come across a place where one creature had crossed the tracks of the other, but it does not happen. There actually seems to be a conscious effort on the part of each type to avoid the other. So why do they continue to live in such close proximity? There are all kinds of theories one could come up with about how one may need the other for some unknown purpose, but at this point, it's impossible to say which, if any, of these theories would be valid.

Whatever the case, it seems likely that events will probably continue in Clearwater County. The sasquatch activity there has roots that go back many years and is still making itself known from time to time. The area is ripe for a major sighting that will come to full public attention. It may happen tomorrow, or it could be years before anyone else sees even a single track, but meanwhile, investigations in the region will continue, and hopefully, some important discoveries can be made.

In the summer of 1995, a severe storm system moved across much of northern Minnesota and produced what turned out to be the worst winds in 200 years. Hurricane-force gales of 85 miles per hour with gusts up to 110 caused massive devastation, and it was this very area that was the hardest hit. So many trees went down that aerial photos of the forest showed what reminded one of the atomic bomb's effects. Loggers moved quickly to clear the forest roads, and there are few obstructions to travel remaining, but much of the forest is still a tangled mess. In this new landscape, the sasquatch must be enjoying a new sense of isolation, sensing that it is now even harder for intruding humans to reach them in their sanctuary- so the hunt has become an even greater challenge.

It seems fitting now to close this account with a few more reflections from Ed Trimble as he looks back at some other incidents from the course of his life that now make him wonder.

For instance, while he has seen hundreds of pairs of animals' eyes reflecting light at night over the years, only once in his life has he seen any that glowed red as the sasquatches are often said to do. This was in the summer of 1942 or 1943 near Lake of the Woods in northwest Minnesota, a pair of dull-red eyes that he and his wife Nova both saw as they drove down a lightly traveled dirt road. First seen at a distance of about 125 yards, the eyes were fairly high off the ground, above the bushes, but at about 25 yards, they disappeared. A trivial event, really, but memorable enough to be recalled decades later, and in that time, Ed has had enough experience to know that he and Nova did not see the eyes of a bear that night.

"September, about 1960... We had been to (a neighbor's place in the Mud Lake area). Nova drove home, I walked the three miles, mostly through wilderness. Came to a clearing- no brush or trees, just grass, area perhaps 60 x 80 feet. That's rare here. The tall grass was all wallowed down flat as though giants had been wrestling or

rolling around on it. It wasn't torn up, I saw no sign of hooved creatures and no manure or scats of any kind. This must have been a
gathering place and playground for some big critters!

"One rather warm fall night in 1965, I was about 25 to 30 feet up in
the crotch of a large aspen tree on a hilltop in our west pasture. I was
roped in so as to avoid falling if I dozed off. The moon was full and
the sky clear. Most of the leaves had fallen and lay dry and crisp. My
rifle hung from a close-by snag. One of our nicest young ewes had
been killed in a draw about a hundred yards east and been dragged to
this hilltop and partly eaten. It was quiet, no breeze that I noticed, no
fox, coyote, skunk, not even a rabbit came close enough for me to
hear on those dry leaves. X dozed fitfully. Suddenly, about 3 AM came
crunch, crunch, crunch, spaced out, sounding just like a man taking
long strides. I strained my eyes, rifle at the ready, but could see nothing. The creature must have matched the fallen leaves in color... it
paused, then resumed, no faster but departing this time. It was not
quite a hundred yards to the fence, which was in good shape and
three and a half feet high. There was no pause in those crunches (at
the fence) and no thump as would be made by jumping over. I knew
next to nothing about Bigfoot types at that time, but now I know that
some of them are said to step over a fence without breaking stride.
The attack and kill had been quick, and I did not suspect coyote. It
wasn't bear work, of that I was sure. I suspected cougar with good
reason but, whatever did it, I now think that this may have been a
close encounter with a Bigfoot!

"Early fall, 1977... A pleasant afternoon for a long hike. Old Sally,
as good a dog as a man could hope to have, and I had been down the
Sugarbush forestry road and back almost to the blacktop highway.
We elected to come home through the woods and had made about a
quarter mile when we heard brush and limbs breaking in the cut-
over area to the south. I thought we might need to backtrack, but as it
neared, it seemed that it'd miss us, so I just crouched down by old Sal,
who behaved perfectly as always. This was a case of curiosity over-
coming fear- on my part. Whatever it was went by at less than 50
yards, but the foliage was so dense I couldn't see it. I had thought

that, for once, I was going to get a close-up look at a moose, or possibly an elk. For some strange reason, I had managed to live in moose country for many years without seeing one, and I still haven't seen one at night. But there was no clatter of hooves on the blacktop highway that was about 200 yards to the north. Neither did we hear any more breaking branches, so I thought that whatever it was had been heading for the fairly open old logging road over there from the start. Bear, except when excited, take the easy way, use paths. Noise doesn't bother them if they are making it themselves wrecking beehives, tearing old logs apart, breaking oak limbs down for acorns, etc. According to what I've recently been reading and hearing, Bigfoot types are quite different in this respect, breaking branches as a sign of their having passed through and, when going on a long journey, going straight through for miles and miles even when going around would be much easier. This experience was exciting. Bigfootish or not, it's absolutely unforgettable!

"December 1988. It was getting late, a mild but cloudy day. Was in a hurry. Neena, our new young dog who didn't do too badly, was along. We were on an old, old logging trail, a spruce bog to our left, a steep, high bank to our right. It was topped with large, beautiful pine timber and had large balsam fir near the base. One of these had gone down and taken smaller conifers with it as it fell. These,

along with its own larger branches propped its trunk up about four feet above the needle-carpeted ground. All of this greenery added up to a snow-covered canopy, perfectly dry underneath. Neena, with her sharp nose, discovered a nice dry bed under there. It was about 3 1/2 feet wide, and five feet long had been used very recently. Tracks led away, but they were mixed in with numerous other tracks; deer, coyote, snowshoe hare, etc. I distinctly recall thinking that those were odd-looking bear tracks, and I remarked about it when I got home. I thought it was the first such bear den I'd ever seen, but there was some question about it. I was not yet into BF lore in 1988.

"I have worked with bees owned by commercial beemen in South Texas, North Dakota, and Minnesota. Have run bees as a hobby in Iowa and commercially during the 1940s in eastern Roseau County near Warroad. We keep a few stands of bees here, too. In this state, at least in the 'wilder' parts of it, if you keep bees, you will sooner or later be aware of bears. I have shot several marauding bears, snared some, and helped conservation men place foot snares and traps for them. I am somewhat familiar with bears on livestock, and not only I, but we are very familiar with how bears go about getting what they want and need from beehives. We have watched them doing it. It's an interesting show but an expensive one. The bear's nose quickly leads it to the best there is in the way of fresh, fragrant honey (carbohydrate), 'bee bread' or stored-up processed pollen (minerals, vitamins, etc.) and brood, the solid slabs of eggs, larvae, and pupae (a rich source of protein, eaten by humans in some cultures). Bruin certainly has a 'sweet tooth' and his stomach expands remarkably. A large one can eat 25 to 30 pounds of this nutritious mixture in a short time, largely ignoring bee stings while doing so but sometimes rubbing and rolling in the grass or weeds and coming right back.

"During the summer of 1990, we had and took care of some typical bear visits to our bee yard. But then we had a strange or unusual occurrence. Some stacks of old, carried-over honey supers were dumped over. Whatever it was that did, it could have gotten into the good, fresh stuff just as easily, for it was only a yard or so away. The damage was slight, the critter went away empty-handed, or I should say empty-stomached. We puzzled over this and referred to it as the most inept, inexperienced, or stupid bear we'd ever heard of. Called it 'that hard-luck bear.'

"Last summer (1991), for the first time in several years, near-normal rainfall came to our area. There were acorns, mushrooms, wild plums, chokecherries, and other wild fruits in abundance, and so bear, and even 'coon weren't much of a problem in cornfields, gardens, etc. But, whatever it was that we had called "Hard Luck" came one day when we weren't home and did the same thing... ignored the easy to get at active colonies, dumped a stack of the old stuff, and filled up on it. We both looked closely at the results and saw no claw marks or tooth marks in the wood and very little breakage. It was most unbearlike, totally non-typical.

"Tim Olson, associate editor of *The Sasquatch Report* that Mike Quast publishes monthly, and I did discover the prints of a small sow bear and her cub, both of which could be called non-typical in that they had only four toes on their feet. That's unheard of until now as far as we have learned, but would they be non-typical in their diet preference? I doubt it, so we, now knowing a bit about the Bigfoot types, suspect that our hard-luck bear isn't a bear!

"June 1990, on our place. On numerous occasions, loggers, fishermen, and campers hang left-over parts of their lunches by a string from a limb. Usually, this prevents loss to wild animals, especially so such undesirables as skunks.

Bear and 'coon and some kinds of squirrels sometimes get wise to it and help themselves. Each of these creatures treat the thin plastic bag differently. The bear bites the bottom of the bag off and eats plastic and all. The others mentioned tear it open, leaving ragged edges. They may sit on the limb eating part of it, but some falls out, and they get down on the ground for that. Once- and only once- I saw where a thin plastic bread bag containing goodies of a sticky nature had been neatly bitten off. The bottom part lay on the ground nearby, turned inside-out and licked off clean. I don't believe that any bear did that!

"Also, last summer (1991), trying hard to meet a deadline, I was on this typewriter until 3 AM... Nova was awake most of that time, too. Three times,

spaced about 30 to 45 minutes apart, we heard a clear, high-pitched call or cry

lasting, she thought, a second or less. I thought a little longer. 'Eeeeeeeeeee.' No variation in tone or loudness. Such a sound is mentioned in John Green's book, 'Sasquatch: The Apes Among Us' in connection with what some tell of hearing while searching for evidence. We can't remember of hearing it before."

Keep your ears open, Ed. You just may hear it again.

The author inspects damage to Ed Trimble's beehives,
the work of something that did not appear to be a bear.

PART III

THE MINNESOTA ICEMAN

19

WHAT YOU ALREADY KNOW

A lot of utter nonsense has been written and said about the Minnesota Iceman. An awful lot. So much so that its' rightful position in the field of cryptozoology has been all but lost and relegated to near comic relief. Writers of fiction, "inspired" by the Iceman, have produced fantastic stories about long-frozen cave men being thawed out and returning to life in today's world. The most recent such effort is 1992's comedy film "Encino Man." All this, despite the fact that the original Iceman (if he was what he appeared to be) had his brains blown out and wasn't about to get up and go anywhere even if he was thawed out.

Being somewhat in charge of investigating creature reports in Minnesota (or at least the only one bothering to do so), I felt it my duty to study the Iceman story, even though the state has only the slightest of claims to it. Its true origins seem to lie half a world away.

Most people who undertake a serious study of the "Bigfoot" phenomenon, reading all they can find about hairy manlike creatures sighted in various parts of the world, will eventually come across the curious case of the Minnesota Iceman. Once they do, depending on their source, they might come to any of several different conclusions about it. Some versions of the story will say that the Iceman was nothing but a dummy made of latex rubber, while others contend it was an actual flesh and blood creature of some kind. Some say there was only one Iceman; others say that there were two or more. The reader will see the opinions of eminent scientists, Bigfoot researchers, and others who were involved, none of whom seem to agree on anything. The study will be a most confusing one, to say the least. So how does one arrive at the truth? It is certainly a case that seems to deserve any researcher's undivided attention, for in it, we supposedly have what Bigfoot people have sought for so many years: the actual corpse of a hair-covered humanoid.

Fact or fancy, the definite points of the Iceman story are as follows:

In 1968 a showman by the name of Frances (Frank) D. Hansen was touring the country, making the rounds of various carnivals and fairs, displaying a sideshow attraction billed, among other names, as the "Siberskoye Creature." What it appeared to be was the corpse of some kind of hairy humanoid frozen in a solid block of ice. Barely any detail was apparent through the cloudy ice, and no one could really be sure of what they were looking at, but nevertheless, the exhibit drew crowds and was quite successful.

In early December of 1968, a Milwaukee herpetologist named Terry Cullen saw the exhibit at the Chicago International Livestock Exposition. Mr. Cullen's primary field of study was reptiles, but he obviously had other interests as well. On December 12th, he phoned Ivan T. Sanderson, then director of the Society for the Investigation of the Unexplained (SITU), and told him what he had seen. The story told by Mr. Hansen, he said, was that the specimen had been found floating in the sea off Siberia by either Russian or Japanese sailors and that he had found it in a refrigeration plant in Hong Kong.

It so happened that Dr. Bernard Heuvelmans, the famous Belgian cryptozoologist, was visiting Sanderson at that time. After considering the potential importance of Cullen's claim, the two decided to travel to Hansen's home near Winona, Minnesota, to examine the specimen.

The examination took place over December 16-18 in a low-ceilinged refrigerated trailer. Hansen refused to allow the specimen to be thawed out or removed from its glass-topped "coffin," thus conditions were far from perfect for a scientific examination, but by shining bright lights on the ice, the two scientists were able to see enough detail for them to take photographs, make detailed drawings, and take measurements of the specimen. They were very impressed by what they saw.

The creature was lying on its back with its right hand resting on its lower abdomen and its left arm thrown up over its head. Its hands were enormous- There appeared to be a break in the left forearm, with protruding bones and some blood visible. There was also blood around the right eye socket. The eyeball was hanging down on the cheek, while the left was missing altogether. The body was covered in dark hair. The face was more or less apelike, but the overall shape of the body was distinctly humanoid. The men naturally suspected a fake at first, but after a time, they both became convinced that they were looking at a real body.

Both men published their findings soon afterward. Heuvelmans excitedly declared that he had inspected a surviving Neanderthal man, giving it the name Homopongoides or the "ape-like man," and called for the opening of a whole new chapter in the study of human evolution. Sanderson was more cautious (somewhat of a switch for him).

He refused to classify the specimen but stated that "it might constitute a very valuable contribution to knowledge and potentially to a better understanding of primate, anthropoid, and possibly hominid ancestry."

Sanderson also alerted John Napier, curator of primates at the prestigious Smithsonian Institution, who expressed cautious interest in what had become commonly known as the Iceman. It all seemed so simple; after years of searching, could the body of a manlike creature just suddenly fall so easily into the hands of science?

Perhaps it was too good to be true, for, at that point, Frank Hansen's Iceman seemed to have undergone a slight change in appearance. This, Hansen explained, was because it had been replaced with a replica that almost, but not quite, duplicated the original. He was not the specimen's real owner, he now claimed. The owner was an anonymous west coast millionaire who had decided to withdraw the original from public display, but the copy would continue to be shown at carnivals.

At a press conference on April 21, 1969, at his farm, Hansen then explained that the Iceman- or Icemen, for he apparently meant both of them- was not real but merely a man-made fabrication. The previous story of its Hong Kong origin was just a typical showman's tall tale, he said. That was all John Napier, and most other scientists needed to hear. Although S. Dillon Ripley, Secretary of the Smithsonian, had been concerned enough to contact the F.B.I. earlier out of worry that the Iceman might be human and the victim of foul play, the Smithsonian now officially dropped all interest in the specimen. Sanderson and Heuvelmans, however, were unconvinced. They were sure they had examined something real.

To confuse the matter even further, an article by Hansen appeared in the July 1970 issue of *Saga* magazine. Entitled "I Killed the Ape-Man Creature of Whiteface," it told how, in 1963, Hansen had been on a hunting trip at the Whiteface Reservoir near Duluth. He was on leave from the Air Force at the time, and while separated from his companions, he shot and wounded a doe which he had to follow. He found it all right, but he also found three hairy man-apes gathered around its carcass, feeding on it. One of them charged Hansen, who hastily shot it through the left eye. The other two fled when their companion went down, and just to be safe, Hansen shot it again in the chest (the Iceman showed signs of both wounds). Weeks later, he returned to the scene to find that the creature's body had been frozen solid by the frigid Minnesota winter. He decided to take it back with him and stored it in a deep freeze until his military service was over, then put it on display. It was not made clear how the anonymous owner fit into this version of the story. After it appeared, most people were pretty well convinced that Hansen was just a showman who never told the same story twice.

And as if that wasn't bad enough, a tabloid called the *National*

Bulletin ran the sensational headline: "I Was Raped by the Abominable Snowman." The story concerned a young woman named Helen Westring who, while hunting alone near Bemidji, was assaulted by the creature, as stated in the headline. During the attack, she fainted, and when she woke up, the beast was still there. She grabbed her fallen rifle and blasted it in the eye, killing it. Supposedly Hansen had then somehow come into possession of the body. As media fiction, the piece was fabulous, but it did nothing to further the study of the Iceman.

The Minnesota Iceman officially died in the spring of 1983, when it was shown for the last time at a car dealership in Rochester. Prior to that, it had not been displayed since August of 1981, when it had come to the end of several years of shopping mall appearances. Despite the fact that it had been declared a fake, people still flocked to see it wherever it went, but after he suffered a heart attack, Frank Hansen decided it was finally time to retire. By that time, the Iceman had long since lost most of its appeal to the Bigfoot community, most of whom accepted the fact that it was indeed just a hoax. But real or fake, where is it today? Indeed, does this question even matter?

Some of the key players in the Iceman saga are no longer with us. Ivan Sanderson died in 1973, and John Napier passed away in 1987. Sanderson never bowed to his critics, who ridiculed his support of the "hoax," maintaining that what he had examined in a cold, cramped trailer in southeast Minnesota had been made of flesh and blood, not rubber. Napier, on the other hand, never saw any reason to accept the Iceman's validity. He said so in his popular 1972 book, "Bigfoot: The Yeti and Sasquatch in Myth and Reality," although in the same book, he admitted his belief in the sasquatch. By the time of his death, he had also been moved to believe in the Himalayan yeti, but not in the Iceman.

Bernard Heuvelmans' mind, too, remains unchanged. Today he is the president of the International Society of Cryptozoology based in Tucson, Arizona, and the director of the Center for Cryptozoology in Le Vesinet, France, where he lives. After a lifetime spent researching unknown and mysterious animals, the Iceman to him stands as one of his greatest discoveries. However, his own version of the creature's origin is radically different from any of the others ever put forth. In a book he co-authored in 1974 with Boris Porshnev, a well-known Russian scientist with similar interests, he reported the findings of his own research and intelligence work. The Iceman was, he states, shot and killed in the jungles of Vietnam and smuggled into the United States on board a U.S. Air Force plane along with a highly illegal cargo of heroin. This bears looking into:

Heuvelmans bases this theory on a number of facts and rumors, primarily the uncovering of a drug ring that did indeed operate during the Vietnam War. They had used the coffins of slain servicemen to smuggle heroin from the "Golden Triangle" of Vietnam, Laos, and Thailand. The airbase at Da Nang was a major point on the smugglers' route. It is also a fact that Frank Hansen served in the Air Force for a time at Da Nang, and he is supposed to have once stated that when he first saw the Iceman, it was in a large plastic bag-similar to a military body bag? (Of course, Hansen has said many other things too, many of which have been dismissed, and it should be made clear that no one is now or has ever accused him of being involved in drug smuggling.)

Furthermore, journalist Jim Lucas wrote for the New York *World Journal Tribune* in November of 1966 that U.S. Marines in the Vietnamese demilitarized zone sometimes shot at jungle tigers and also had, on one occasion, "shot a huge ape." Since there are no known great apes in Vietnam this sounds quite suspicious, and Heuvelmans had also heard persistent rumors about the killing of a "wild hairy man" in South Vietnam.

All of this served as circumstantial evidence for Heuvelmans' theory, but there appears to be no documentation to link it all together or to prove that it forms the origin of the Minnesota Iceman. Still, he contends that the creature is no sasquatch. Rather it is what he always insisted it was- a member of a race of Neanderthal men that survives in Asia to this day.

Could Heuvelmans' theory be true? It is certainly no more

outlandish than some of the other origins put forth for the enigmatic
Iceman.

Drawing taken from a photograph in the well-
known Gordon Yeager article "'Ice Man' Not
Real, but Murky Mystery is Left" on April 21,
1969, Rochester *Post-Bulletin*. This would be
the phony Iceman, with Frank Hansen standing
at the head.

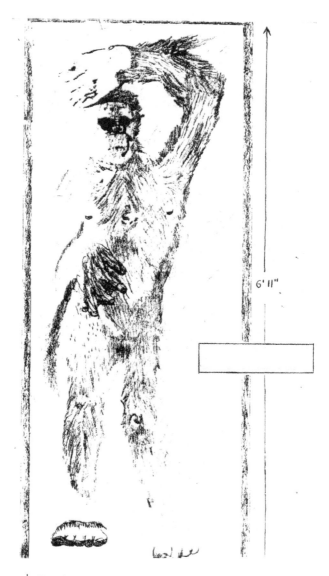

6' 11"

Drawing based on one of Ivan Sanderson's
illustrations of the real Iceman.

20

THE TRUTH

I t is very, very unfortunate that the Iceman came to be involved with show business. If things had gone differently, I think the whole subject of hairy manlike creatures would be viewed far differently today, for the better. But he's gone now, and personally, I don't think he'll ever reappear. It's just possible, but don't hold your breath.

The whole Iceman issue, for most people, is just as confused today as it ever was. Why is this so? one might ask. Any child can see that the obvious way to settle the problem has got to be to simply go to the Iceman's owner, melt the ice, and see what's inside. Even if he refused, one would think that it would have been done illegally behind his back by someone in all this time, right?

But unfortunately, it is not as simple as that. The owner's name has never been revealed, nor has the present location of the Iceman.

So the question stands: isn't there anyone who knows the truth?

The answer to that, too, should be obvious: Frank D. Hansen himself.

Many investigators would totally dismiss any and all of Hansen's claims purely on the basis of his past behavior, regarding him as a useless source of information, but he is not a showman anymore. Today he lives quietly on his farm a mile or so from the tiny town of

Altura, Minnesota, no longer bothered by the endless attention that was his all those years ago. (Almost all previous accounts give his address as "near Winona," which is the nearest city of greater size-Altura is just harder to find on the map.) He is retired from the carnival business now, with no more need to make up conflicting reports to draw attention. Indeed, it is peace and quiet he seeks now.

I visited him in July of 1989. He had never heard of me, didn't know I was coming, and had no time to make up anything new, but in the very spot where Sanderson and Heuvelmans had made their famous inspection, he sat down with me and told me all he now has to say about the Minnesota Iceman.

Some call the Iceman by the name "Bozo," a carnival clown, nothing more. To most serious investigators now, that's all he was- a phony, no more real than a mannequin. He has, for the most part, been written off as a big joke. But the joke is on them because the Iceman was real.

Hansen's story, as told now, begins in 1963. As he stated in his *Saga* article, he was serving in the Air Force at Duluth when he went on a hunting trip to the nearby Whiteface Reservoir. He will not go into detail about what he saw during that hunt, only that it was "a strange phenomenon... maybe it was from outer space, maybe it was Bigfoot, I don't know." He does say that he saw a creature of some kind and that the Air Force has it on record that a UFO landing took place over the area at that time, and also that if I cared to track down his hunting companions, they would attest to the frightened state his encounter put him in.

Four years later, his military service was over, and he was in the carnival business, displaying an antique tractor that he owned. (The Winona Historical Society has news clippings on file about this.) At the 1967 Arizona State Fair, he met a man who to this day he will not name, but he says, "It was a name I recognized immediately," and that it was someone connected to the entertainment industry. The man said he had a very interesting specimen in storage in California and asked Hansen to consider taking it on a carnival tour. Shortly after that, in Long Beach, Hansen first laid eyes on the Iceman.

The man explained that an agent of his had discovered the creature in its frozen state in a refrigeration plant in Hong Kong and that it had originally been found floating in the sea by Chinese fishermen in a 6,000-pound ice block. He was a deeply religious man, he explained, and he thought this creature seemed to go against the theory of creation as told in the Bible; thus, he wanted no connection to it. Hansen agreed to display it, but first, the ice was temporarily shaved down for his benefit, and he saw that it was indeed a real corpse, not a fake.

Hansen was given permission to use whatever phony advertising he wished in order to draw crowds. Stories about "Bigfoot" in the news at that time helped as well, and the display was very popular.

One of the ad campaigns was particularly amusing. Hansen's antique tractor display had used a sign reading something like "Found in the woods of Minnesota," meaning that he had found and restored the tractor. He now took the same sign and attached it to the Iceman trailer for some of its appearances. (Hansen showed me another large sign, still stored today in his barn, reading "Is it Prehistoric?" that once adorned the display.)

After some time, though, Hansen began to worry that he might get into serious legal trouble if what he had turned out to be a human corpse. So, returning to California, he had a replica manufactured from latex rubber and hair, intending to switch it with the original if he ever had to. A man often mentioned in connection with this model is Howard Ball, who was in the business of making such things for the movie industry. Hansen says that it was Ball who began the project, but he took it elsewhere when he was not satisfied with the way it was turning out. A number of model-making companies have claimed to be the creators of the Iceman over the years. In fact, they may all be telling the truth, for Hansen brought the project to several different experts before he was satisfied that he had a good enough likeness of the original. (The claims of the model makers are what many skeptics use to totally dismiss the Iceman as a hoax and nothing more.)

The reports published by Sanderson and Heuvelmans brought an incredible amount of attention to Hansen's way, much to his anger because he had insisted on no publicity when he allowed them to examine the Iceman. He was particularly upset with Heuvelmans, whose report appeared first.

According to Hansen, what does not appear in either scientist's report is just how they became convinced the Iceman was real. To get the best possible view of it, they had hung bright lights over the glass under which it lay, and while Hansen was away from them for a moment, one of them placed one of the hot lights directly on the ice-cold glass. It shattered, and a pungent odor like that of rotting flesh rose from the ice. This convinced them that an actual corpse, freshly killed, lay before them. Hansen will never forget what the distinguished scientists said when he reminded them of their promise not to publicize the story at that point. "We are scientists first," they told him, "and gentlemen second." (He doesn't say exactly which

Most sources today report that J. Edgar Hoover, head of the F.B.I., officially informed the Smithsonian that he saw no reason for his Bureau to become involved in investigating the Iceman, but according to Hansen, after the story broke, he was indeed visited by federal agents from nearby Rochester. As further advertisement, a sign reading "Investigated by the F.B.I." later began appearing on the Iceman display, but the Bureau's interest was exactly the kind of thing Hansen had feared.

And so, one night, he loaded up the Iceman in a truck and drove off with it. He went south and met the owner in a secret location to turn it over to him. He hasn't seen it since and to this day has no idea where it is.

(Interestingly, he says that during this brief trip, he was detained by police in Iowa for a short time who never knew what he had in the back of his truck.)

The replica took the Iceman's place at that point, and to further discredit the notion that anything real had ever been involved, Hansen came out with the *Saga* article, basing it on his sighting of a strange beast five years earlier in 1963 and altering it to say that he had killed the creature.

Today Hansen possesses neither the original nor the replica Iceman, although he is aware of others who have tried to cash in with their own inferior copies. He thinks of the whole affair as a learning experience that taught him much about his fellow men. He also told me that day in 1989 that he does not much care what anyone says about the case because, for him, at least, it is a thing of the past.

Not too much had been said or written about the Minnesota Iceman for several years when, on September 25, 1994, the NBC television show "Unsolved Mysteries" featured a story about it which went over most of the basic story as it was already known, with actors portraying Frank Hansen and the other central figures. Mark A. Hall was featured, giving his more or less positive opinions on the case.

He happened to have taken some of the most widely distributed photos of the original Iceman back in the 60s, although he seldom gets credit for it. I was watching a videotaped story about it with him once when he pointed and said, "I think I took that picture."

Terry Cullen was also featured. He explained how he had been so amazed by the exhibit in Chicago that he'd gone back several times to examine it more closely and that Hansen had seemed to grow suspicious of his frequent visits. Meanwhile, he was trying to find a qualified expert to come and view it, but none were interested in such sideshow attractions. Finally, an anthropologist from the University of Minnesota agreed to look at it, and according to Cullen, he came out of the exhibit in a daze and just said, "It's amazing," and walked away. It was after that that Cullen called Ivan Sanderson. This was the only part of the story I hadn't heard before.

(Coincidentally, Prof. Grover Krantz, a noted authority on the sasquatch and one of the few scientists who gives the subject any attention, went to school at the U of M and commented in his book "Big Footprints" that if he had walked just a little farther at one particular carnival, he would have been the first scientist to see the Iceman, which he believes was real.)

"Unsolved Mysteries" stated that Hansen had been asked to participate in their broadcast but that he had declined. This didn't surprise me since he had said he wanted nothing to do with the case anymore.

I wrote about the show in *The Sasquatch Report* newsletter.

Shortly after that, I got a surprise when Hansen himself gave me a call. Someone had apparently sent him a copy of the newsletter, and he had a few comments to make about the whole thing. He had declined to take part in the show, he said, because he hadn't cared for the way it was being done, not because he was being reclusive or had anything to hide.

But the biggest surprise came when he said that he had recently heard from the real owner of the Iceman, who he had not talked to in a long time and didn't even know if the man was still living. He still wouldn't name him, of course, but he said the owner claimed to still be in possession of the original Iceman and that it was still frozen and in good condition. Also, he might (just might) consider presenting it to the public once again in the near future.

Well, that was a couple of years ago. No word yet.

Terry Cullen had also appeared at a cryptozoology conference hosted by Grover Krantz in Pullman, Washington, in June of 1989 and publicly stated that he still felt the Iceman was most probably genuine. He said he was not trying to change anyone's mind, but several people said they got that impression anyway.

Bernard Heuvelmans, meanwhile, states that while the Iceman saga has been described in many publications over the years, "...it has never been described correctly [except] in my own book."

However, the last word belongs to that anonymous owner, who once stated to Hansen that if he was ever identified, he would dump the Iceman in the Pacific Ocean.

If the Iceman was indeed real, then, just what was it? There are many who would like to connect it with the North American sasquatch, but it is unlikely that such a connection exists.

For the most part, I believe what Frank Hansen told me about the Iceman being discovered by the fishermen. Based on this and other facts, I believe the creature was a specimen of what is commonly known as "Ye-Ren" or Chinese Wildmen. These creatures have been sighted in the mountains of China for generations, and although they are little known in America, they have just as interesting a history as our own sasquatch. Some investigators think they may be a surviving species of Neanderthal man, just as Heuvelmans has theorized. The Chinese government has funded major scientific expeditions to search for them, which is more effort than the sasquatch has ever been given. There was also a search by Dr. Frank Poirer of Ohio and Richard Greenwell, secretary of the International Society of Crypto-zoology, which turned up impressive evidence to support the existence of the wildman. To the north, in Mongolia and the former Soviet Union, similar creatures have been given the name Almas in some regions, Kaptar in others. These areas are not too far removed from the Himalayas, where the yeti or "Abominable Snowman" has gained such fame, but descriptions seem to make that creature out to be considerably less manlike in appearance and nature.

How one of these creatures came to be floating in a three-ton

ice block in the open sea after sustaining what appeared to be gunshot wounds is anyone's guess and would probably make an even more interesting story than the Iceman made after arriving in America.

Where is the Iceman now? Will it ever be revealed? Who killed it? Who is its mysterious owner? Unfortunately, many questions remain. In time perhaps they will be answered, but for now, the poor creature appears to be resting in peace.

The trailer in which the Iceman was displayed in the late 1960s, photographed in July of 1989 at Frank Hansen's farm outside of Altura, Minnesota.

PART IV

THE DAKOTAS

21

NORTH DAKOTA - NOT MUCH GOING ON

I f you enjoy wide-open spaces, North Dakota is the place for you. If it's deep woods you're looking for, though, you'll have to go elsewhere.

Many people joke about North Dakota being the most ultimately boring state in America, and indeed, a drive across it finds most routes pretty featureless and extremely flat. Natives of the state, however, will defend it with great zeal.

Tourism campaigns for North Dakota rely heavily on its colorful history (it is rich in American Indian lore and was one of the old stomping grounds of Teddy Roosevelt and the home of General George Armstrong Custer) and on the extreme western end of the state. Here lies the famous Badlands, with their vast stretches of cliff faces and magnificent, colorful rock formations unique to this area. Here, one can also visit the Little Missouri National Grassland and Theodore Roosevelt National park and see more buffalo than you are likely to see anywhere else.

As another note of interest, before the end of the Cold War, it was once implied that if North Dakota ever withdrew from the Union, it would be one of the largest nuclear powers in the world. The open prairie has a lot of room for missile silos.

Virtually nowhere, though, are there any really large expanses of forest, and so it comes as no great surprise that the sasquatch appears to have been very seldom seen there. The few reports that do exist are quite far between.

In 1967 a Mrs. Myrtle Paschen wrote to investigator Roger Patterson to tell the story of a sighting shortly after the turn of the century in the Killdeer Mountains area of western North Dakota. (These mountains only rise to just over 3,000 feet.) Some people in a sleigh reportedly saw a gorilla-like animal that ran toward them at first and then fled, leaving manlike tracks in the snow.

The October 1990 issue of the *Bigfoot Co-Op* related the following, quoting the December 18, 1989 edition of the *Rocky Mountain News*:

"(Ron) Brienzo, 40, lives in Houston and is a high school English teacher by profession. He has searched for Bigfoot through the Louisiana bayous, the forest of the Northwest, and the flanks of Pike's Peak for more than 20 years.

"He thinks he might have seen a Bigfoot once in North Dakota along the Canadian border after he followed 21-inch footprints sunk more than an inch into [the] frozen ground. He wrecked a snowmobile, trying to catch up to the dark, shaggy, upright animal. He thinks he heard it once, a sound between a big cat's cry and the call of a woman or a baby."

Unfortunately, this article listed no date or exact location for the incident.

The famous outburst of sasquatch sightings on the Standing Rock Indian Reservation in 1977 will be covered in full shortly. Part of the reservation lies in North Dakota and part in South Dakota, but as you will see, only one of the many sightings occurred in North Dakota, that being along the Cannonball River along the reservation's northern border.

Apart from that, all the rest we have for this state appeared in an article in the November 14, 1979, *Spokane Daily Chronicle*, supplied to me by investigator John Green:

WAS IT GORILLA OF HIS DREAMS?

Werner, ND- It was dark, about 7 p.m. last October 26, when the two Dunn County men traveled around a curve on a road a mile south of Werner.

They were in the wide-open stretches of west-central North Dakota, heading to town. Their pickup truck's headlights shone on a dark object standing at the road's edge.

"I had to swerve to miss it," said the driver. He asked not to be identified.

"Did you see that Black Angus calf we almost hit?" the driver said he casually asked his companion.

"That was no Black Angus calf," he said, his passenger replied. "That was an ape, a Bigfoot."

"That's what I thought," the driver said he excitedly replied.

The men stopped the pickup and sat a few minutes, discussing what they had seen. They went back for a second look.

Shining the truck lights into the ditch and nearby fields, they saw nothing. Whatever it was had disappeared.

"The object had looked like an ape," the driver said. "Shaggy."

"When we passed it, it threw its arms up like this," he said, holding his arms wide and pointing slightly forward.

The driver said the object was a "big gorilla, twice the size of a man." He estimated its height at six to seven feet. "It had awful long, stringy hair, almost down to its waist."

He couldn't distinguish facial features or see any fingers. The hair was "like ropes hanging from its head to its waist." It was "grayish-black in color."

The driver said last Friday, he returned to the area about two days after the sighting. He searched for tracks. He found none.

A check of the area, from Killdeer to Halliday, turned up three other unusual, unconfirmed sightings.

A Halliday-area man, one source said, claimed he saw a Bigfoot two weeks earlier north of Halliday. He refused to report it until he heard the story of the two men in the pickup.

The pickup driver said he would have remained silent if he hadn't had a passenger to back up his description of what he saw.

A check with game warden Bill Schaller of Halliday revealed that a huge black moose was seen three times in the Killdeer Mountain area between Oct, 1 and Oct, 10.

The pickup driver said, "It wasn't a moose. I know what we saw."

Schaller said Saturday, a Grassy Butte ranch woman said she saw a bear in her garden one morning last February.

There is one final story that could be included, but it is completely undocumented.

Sometimes it truly helps just to know the right people. In talking to a friend-of-a-friend just briefly one day, a person I've only met once, the subject of my sasquatch interest came up, and he casually mentioned how his grandparents near Devil's Lake, North Dakota, claimed that one of the creatures had once thrown dirt in the window of their house. He was short on other details. I suppose it makes sense that most of these North Dakota reports are from the western portion of the state, where the most rugged terrain lies. All in all, though, it's not much of a showing, and while there probably are a few sasquatches somewhere in North Dakota, at least at times, there are many much better places to go searching for them.

22

SOUTH DAKOTA INCIDENTALS

M ount Rushmore. Black Hills Gold. Badlands National Park. The world's largest annual motorcycle rally (Sturgis).

And sometimes- sasquatch.

All of these are features of the state of South Dakota, which differs in many ways from its sister state to the north. East of the Missouri River, the two are similar in topography, with mile upon mile of rolling prairie, but to the west, South Dakota becomes a surface of buttes, ravines, and canyons, as well as the occasional wide expanse of forest that increase in ruggedness toward the Badlands and the Black Hills. With points over 7,000 feet in elevation, these hills are the highest land in the U.S. east of the Rockies and have always been considered sacred ground by the Sioux Indians.

Old West lore flourishes in South Dakota. Oddly, though, its wilderness appears to have produced no publicized reports of the sasquatch until as late as 1973.

In November of that year, three men on a forest service road near Johnson Siding in the Black Hills saw in their headlights what they described as a 10-foot shaggy, dirty-white creature. It picked up a dead deer under one arm and crashed into the underbrush.

In that same year, also in the Black Hills, Daniel Tweten found what he feels just might have been a possible sasquatch footprint beside a stream while searching an old gold mining camp for artifacts. Dan is from Clearwater County, Minnesota (see chapter 14 for his encounters with strange tracks there), but at that time, he spent his spare time in South Dakota exploring the old mines.

The Black Hills National Forest seems to be popular with the creatures. In March of 1974, two young boys near the small town of Nemo saw on a hill near their home a large, heavy-set, human-shaped beast covered with orange-brown hair.

Taking a big jump all the way over to the southeast corner of the state, a second report came out of 1974 near the town of Jefferson. On September 6th, Mr. Jim Douglas was driving when he saw a sandy-colored creature standing nine feet tall dragging a red furry object through an alfalfa field. It stopped for a time to stand and watch him.

In the Summer of 1977 near Spearfish, at the northern edge of the Black Hills National Forest, Betty Johnson and her daughters Brenda, Bonnie, and Becky saw two sasquatches eating in a cornfield. One was from seven to eight feet tall with black hair, the other smaller and brownish-red with a black face. These creatures made a whistling sound.

There was an unusual report in September of 1979 near Bruce on the east side of the state. Witnesses Jeff Anderson, Carrie Williams, and one other, all 13 years old, said they had seen a monkey-like animal on several occasions. It was 2 1/2 to three feet tall, was brownish in color, and had big ears but no tail. It ran very fast on two legs, but one of the boys managed to get to within 20 feet of it, giving him an excellent view of it. Was it a baby sasquatch?

Another eastern report came from the Rauville area near Watertown. On October 22, 1979, a man and his wife saw a five-foot creature with dark red eyes sitting beside Highway 81. Other sightings of four to five-foot black creatures were also reportedly made in the area.

Ed Trimble, always a dedicated collector of sasquatch stories, heard about a South Dakota sighting from some people who knew the witness and checked into it himself. He wrote the following account:

"Hank Armstrong is a long-distance trucker. Between long hauls, Hank likes to take [his] wife and family down southeast into the Pine Ridge Indian Reservation, where they are well acquainted. There, south of Badlands National Park, north of the historic Wounded Knee site, and near the town of Porcupine, they go in a four-wheel-drive vehicle (which, Hank says, is necessary), taking a picnic lunch and watching for antelope, prairie dogs, and other wildlife.

"On one such trip during fall 1989, Hank, his wife, their daughter, and his wife's cousin had quite a surprise. As he recalls, it was about 1:30 or 2:00 p.m. on an overcast day, the temperature around 45 and wind about 30 mph. This, for that season and place, is not unusual. They were just about to cross a low spot when, ahead and to one side, they all saw an upright, dark reddish-brown creature standing at an estimated distance of 100 yards. It was seven or eight feet tall and had a pointy head. It started to run fast toward a dry watercourse lined with cottonwood trees. Upon crossing the brief low spot, they could no longer see it. They thought that anything that big would surely leave tracks but were unable to find any.

"The people of Porcupine told of having often noticed a very musky odor and said that the village dogs that usually roamed widely always returned when this was noticeable. An unusual scream was also reported in connection with the odor. This went on for a period of about six months. Hank doesn't know of any other sightings or incidents since then."

You may recall "Bob," the 1960 witness from Clearwater County, Minnesota (see chapter 14). While telling me about his own sighting, he mentioned that he had heard about sasquatches being seen on the Pine Ridge Reservation in southwestern South Dakota, I believe sometime in the late 1980s, which would correlate with the Armstrong sighting. He was short on specifics, but he recalled that the Indians at that time had been afraid to go outside because of the creatures.

This area was also briefly mentioned, you may remember, in the newspaper article on Prairie Island, Minnesota's "Big Man" (see chapter one).

And in a noteworthy coincidence, the notorious massacre at Wounded Knee on Pine Ridge on December 29, 1890, included the death of an Indian leader named Chief Bigfoot.

Finally, a man from Wagner, South Dakota (initials B.D.) who told Tim Olson about a friend of his from Ely, Minnesota who'd seen a sasquatch (see chapter two) had himself seen footprints and possibly heard the creatures' sounds somewhere in the Black Hills. These reports are all interesting, but the story everyone remembers from South Dakota that overshadows all the rest is told in the next chapter.

23

THE LITTLE EAGLE EPISODE

The second half of 1977 is a time destined to be remembered for decades to come by the people of the Standing Rock Indian Reservation on the northern border of South Dakota. That was when reporters from across the nation descended on the tiny town of Little Eagle, population 300, and gave it a few brief moments of national fame.

The reason for all the excitement was that a small group of wayward sasquatches seemed to have staked a claim in the area at that time, and everyone wanted to know about them.

In all, there were 28 sightings from August to December. It was a most remarkable situation, the kind a sasquatch hunter dreams of, but once it was over, nothing had really changed except for serious attention being given to the question of sasquatch reports in mid-America.

It all began in the summer in the area of Red Scaffold, where a young girl had to be treated at a hospital after being terrified by a "foul-smelling, hairy creature" while she was home alone.

On August 9th, near Green Grass, three policemen saw a six to seven-foot apelike creature at 3 AM. It was moving along a creek bottom, observed by a spotlight beam.

In mid-August, two sightings occurred along the Grand River. Two boys, Todd and Chad Alexander (ages 12 and 9), were riding horses when they saw the "long hairy legs" of an upright animal, the rest of the body obscured by bushes. A few days later, Craig Two Hearts (16) saw a huge hairy animal a quarter mile away while he was repairing a house.

So far, these could have been isolated incidents, but it was only the beginning.

In mid-September, Chris Howiatow and some other people were checking some cattle when a "big ape" watched them from a hillside. They went toward it, but it ran into some brush.

At around the same time, a report came from across the border in North Dakota. Paul Monzelowsky (60) and his son were looking for a stray bull when they saw an animal "like a big monkey" standing eight or nine feet tall (a big monkey indeed!). They chased it in their pickup, but it ran "as fast as a horse" and leaped a creek near the Cannonball River.

On September 28th, east of town, Nancy Chasing Hawk, Esther Thundershield, and Myron Fast Horse heard howling sounds outside, turned on the headlights of a truck, and saw a tall, hairy animal with green eyes run into some brush.

Also that month, Lemar Chasing Hawk saw a nine-foot sasquatch in some bushes that frightened him into running home.

In October, the sightings increased even more. Phoebe Little Dog (58) saw a creature north of Little Eagle on October 6th.

On October 13th, southeast of Little Eagle (evidence that the town was literally surrounded by this activity), Cecilia Thundershield, Dan Uses Arrow, and Albert Dog had a sighting. Cecilia and Dan saw a creature come from some woods. They went and got Albert, who saw it go back into the woods. It had long arms almost to its knees and walked in a slouched position.

That same day, Phoebe Little Dog saw a creature again in a cattle pasture, the same location as her earlier sighting a week before, and also that day, Lyle Maxon (48) heard a "funny scream... either a bobcat or the creature" near Little Eagle at 1:30 a.m.

On October 22nd, along the Grand River, four men on horseback saw a sasquatch basking in the sun in a field. It ran away from them, and though they searched, they could not relocate it.

Three days later, on the 25th, near the Grand River Bridge at Little Eagle, Alwin Ducheneaux saw a creature in the beam of headlights at about midnight.

A major sighting on October 29th involved Bureau of Indian Affairs police officer Verdell Veo, his son Jeff Veo (15), another teenage son, and officers Bobby Gates and Selvin Arlen. They were on Elkhorn Buttes northeast of Little Eagle when they spotted a creature in the moonlight, and two of the men started to walk toward it. Veo had a strange feeling that there was no weapon that would have worked against the eight to nine-foot beast. He said, "Something told me- I could sense it if you can understand- that I'd better just get out of there and leave the thing alone." As the men started back, then, Jeff rushed toward them and shouted that a second creature was also present. He had watched it walking along behind the men through an infrared rifle scope.

That same night on a ranch northwest of Timber Lake, Albert and Deleen Kougl were awakened by an eerie sounding cry outside their home that they heard three times. Mr. Kougl pounded on the wall, and the sounds ceased. The next day Sheriff Ted Schweitzer found large footprints outside the Kougl home.

Late in the month at Little Eagle, Irene Village Center saw a creature in some marshy brush.

These four sightings occurred at various times throughout the fall:

Near LaPlant, a bit south of Little Eagle, Melvin Garreaux saw a creature, and its tracks were then found by Verdell and Jeff Veo.

On a bluff overlooking the town of Little Eagle, Hanna Shooting Bear (70) looked out her kitchen window one night at about ten o'clock and saw a large hairy creature looking through a window of her daughter's trailer home about 30 yards away. She described it as having a "funny big head, almost as though it had horns and wide shoulders. Its arms were up, and the hands curled down, and it swayed back and forth." She sent her dogs outside after it, but they were afraid and crawled under a car. Hanna ran to the trailer to alert the occupants, but by then, the creature had moved off. Her son-in-law fired several rifle shots into the air to make sure it stayed away. Hanna was of the opinion that the creature was dangerous and should be killed. (This sighting became one of the most publicized.)

In another part of the reservation, Mr. and Mrs. Walter Chasing Hawk were driving at night and saw green eyes shining in their head-lights. Walter thought it might be a deer, so he got out with his rifle, but then he saw that it was a sasquatch standing eight feet tall. Police searched the scene but found nothing.

Back at the Grand River, Mrs. Angus Long Elk saw a creature by the river.

In November, things showed no signs of letting up. On the night of the 5th, Verdell Veo was again involved. He and several others, including rancher Gary Alexander chased a sasquatch for several hours. It was surrounded by vehicles, illuminated by many head-lights, but still, it managed to escape and hide itself in the brush. Alexander said he heard the sound of running feet and what sounded like someone out of breath. "I put my flashlight right where I could plainly hear it, only where it should have been there was nothing in sight! Now what I'm wondering is, can this thing make itself invisible when things get too close for comfort?"

Well, this was the only report of anything like that, so perhaps Alexander was just a little disoriented by all the excitement.

On November 13th, north of Little Eagle, a male driver saw a crea-ture on the road and was so startled that he drove into the ditch.

On the 23rd, about a dozen women and children decided to try and lure the creatures by having a nocturnal campfire party at Little Eagle. Two creatures were seen crouching in some brush near the fire.

Things finally started to slack off after that, but there were three final sightings in December:

On the third, Gary Alexander was again involved. He and two others, Lowell and Keith Olson, watched two creatures for three minutes. One was eight to *8 1/2* feet tall and dark in color, the other a foot shorter. This was on Elkhorn Buttes.

Also, on the Buttes, Verdell Veo had another sighting on December 5th. He also saw two creatures together.

Finally, in a sighting again involving Gary Alexander, he and some other people were out snowmobiling when they saw two creatures that looked at them but did not run away.

That was it. As suddenly as it had begun, this strange episode finally faded away.

Apart from the sightings, there were also incidents of track finds that, together with the eyewitness descriptions, seemed to indicate the presence of at least three individual creatures on the reservation, probably all adults. (A possible juvenile track was seen only once and could have been that of a human.) It was theorized that they may have been traveling east and become trapped in the area for a time when they couldn't find a way across long and winding Lake Oahe, which forms the eastern border of Standing Rock. Sasquatches are usually regarded as good swimmers, however, so this theory may or may not have merit.

The Lakota people of Standing Rock are said to have called their mysterious visitors "Taku He," which means simply "What is it?" In contrast to the usual spiritual attitude that American Indians commonly have toward the sasquatch, these particular people seem to have reacted with great surprise and no small amount of fear to the creatures' presence. No one got hurt, though, and all that was really to fear was probably the encroachment of the white man into their simple lifestyles during this brief and unwanted moment of stardom.

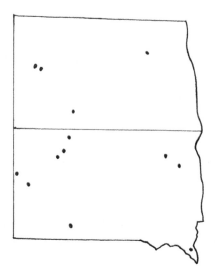

Locations of sasquatch reports in North and South Dakota.

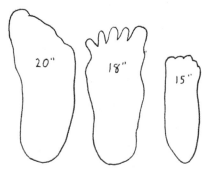

Footprints found in the Little Eagle area in 1977 indicating the presence of three individual creatures. It may have been a family group, but even the smallest print is easily big enough to be that of an adult. Photos appeared in articles at the time showing casts of the 20" and 18" prints, with policeman Verdell Veo holding the former. (A 10" print was also seen once, but it could have been human.)

You've just read about scores of separate incidents in Minnesota and the Dakotas involving encounters with what appeared to be large, hairy, manlike, or apelike creatures. The majority of these reports come from perfectly reliable everyday people who have shown no desire to profit in any way from their stories or any other reason why they should be considered liars. I hope you find truth in these claims, but that is up to you.

As for me, when I am asked, "Do you believe in the sasquatch?" I find it an almost absurd question. To say that you "believe in" something is to admit to its dubious nature. I am as convinced that the sasquatch exists as I am of the existence of any other animal. I have seen one, I have seen their tracks, I believe I've heard their voices, and I have spoken with many others who have done the same.

For me, there is absolutely no doubt whatsoever.

I have tried, in my research and investigations, to put everything into some sort of order and to establish the exact range of these creatures, their population, the best time of year to look for them- any kind of useful pattern. Others have also tried this and are still trying, even using computers for the meticulous study of reports. At this point, however, I have realized that there are no easy answers to these questions. Just when you think you've established a pattern, a new report comes along that shatters it. But there are some things that do seem clear:

The sasquatch is an animal, not a human being. Some believe the creatures are another species of man because of their upright posture, but a penguin also walks upright, and no one thinks of it as human. Most sasquatches have a very humanlike foot, but that does not make them human either. Everything else about them is much more apelike than manlike. Presently science accepts the chimpanzee as our closest living relative, but no one thinks chimps are actually human. I think full acceptance of the sasquatch would drop the chimp to number two, but they will both still be classified as animals. (Technically, of course, man himself is really an "animal," but we use the term in a more convenient manner.)

The argument rages over whether or not it is morally right to kill a sasquatch to prove they exist. Many people react with great sympathy for the creatures, saying, "Well, they've never hurt anyone. What right do we have to kill them?" But these same people are often avid hunters who regularly go out and kill many other animals that have never hurt anyone either. Whatever decision one makes on this issue, I don't think it should be based on an emotional reaction to the possibility of the sasquatch being human.

I am not here to tell people how to proceed in this business, nor to judge whether they are right or wrong to stalk the sasquatch with guns. Whatever we end up doing with this animal, though, we can be assured that we are dealing with a quite non-human primate.

Another obvious point is that these animals are not confined to the Pacific Northwest as was once believed. To my knowledge, the only areas of the United States and Canada with no sasquatch reports on record are Hawaii, Rhode Island, and Nova Scotia. Some states and provinces have only a few while others have hundreds, but clearly, the sasquatch is a very wide-ranging animal. The idea put forth by those most opposed to killing one- that they are an endangered species- is obviously false. There must be an awful lot of them out there, and they certainly aren't being overhunted.

This raises an interesting point: I have expended just as much thought in dealing with the misconceptions of believers as I have with those of skeptics! But it is still the skeptics' arguments that are the most fun to tackle. For instance:

"North America's climate cannot support primates."

This is disproven by the existence of Japanese snow monkeys and of langurs in the high Himalayas, to name just a couple. And the idea of a North American primate is really not even all that remarkable. They exist in South America, Asia, and Africa, so why not here?

"North American's forests could never support an animal of such size."

Really? Try telling that to any self-respecting grizzly bear, moose, or elk, all of which are as big or bigger than the sasquatch.

"If they exist, why don't we find their bones?"

This one has been beaten down so many times it's almost redundant now, but people still say it. The fact is that we don't find the bones of anything else very often either. I challenge anyone— go out in the woods and look for a raccoon's skeleton. Then call me in twenty years when you still haven't found one. Nature has a natural disposal system that does away with most dead bodies very quickly. Roadkills are common enough, of course, and hunters' kills are sometimes left behind, but as for <u>natural deaths</u> in the wild — happy hunting.

(And despite all this, there <u>are</u> a few stories of possible sasquatch bones being found, but that's another long story.)

And finally, the most laughable question asked by skeptics:

"If they really exist, why aren't they seen more often?"

Obviously- THEY ARE!

I think there could be 10,000 sightings, and 10,000 times that question would be seriously asked. Therefore I will continue working to help bring about the day when the existence of these North American primates is proven beyond doubt to everyone the world over, and I encourage others to do the same.

I feel that labeling the sasquatch a "monster" early on was one of the most unfortunate circumstances imaginable. That word throws up immense psychological roadblocks in the path of serious study.

No one but small children believe in monsters, so what scientist will spend time and money looking for one? But this is not a "monster hunt." It is an important zoological pursuit.

Vampires, werewolves, demons- <u>those</u> are monsters (if one chooses to believe in such things).

We're dealing with a truly remarkable animal here, and many people are living their entire lives believing it's nothing but a laughable myth. What a sad thing that is.

APPENDIX A: CROOKSTON - BIGFOOT CAPITAL OF THE WORLD

E xcuse me, but last I heard, it was Willow Creek, California, that held the unofficial title of Bigfoot Capital of the World, and with their history, they surely deserve it.

Thus it came as quite a surprise when I saw the first news clippings about the city of Crookston, Minnesota, and its plans to set itself up as a sort of "sasquatch central," especially since the area was a total blank on my map of sasquatch reports.

One article in the Minneapolis *Star Tribune* for July 6, 1995, quoted Don Holbrook of the Crookston Economic Development Authority as saying, "We're not just doing it as a hoax... We're going to do some more research on Minnesota sightings." However, it went on to say that he was "not aware of any specific locations where Bigfoot may have been seen in the state."

Having a file fairly overflowing with Minnesota reports, I could only assume that Mr. Holbrook hadn't been looking very hard. I wrote to him, offering my services as a serious investigator, but when I got no reply, I thought the project had probably amounted to very little.

Some months later, it was back in the news, however, and perhaps the whole story is best told in a pamphlet that is offered by the city of Crookston:

"It all began in the summer of 1995, the middle of June to be exact.

"The city editor from the Crookston Daily Times was talking to the executive director of the Crookston Development Authority one afternoon about a possible story relating to a possible future development in town.

"The two enjoyed sitting around and chewing the fat with each other, so when the interview was over, the executive director told the city editor of his idea for a potential future tourist attraction in town centered around none other than the famous Bigfoot.

"The executive director had done his homework and had several specifics already worked out. Crookston's Bigfoot would have its own identity and would be known as the Plains Bigfoot, or to commoners, the Field Running Bigfoot. He was known to be seen running with the moose east of town, the executive director said.

"In the June 20 edition of the Times, a story written by the city editor appeared with a large headline saying: Bigfoot sighted? In it, he described the executive director's radical plan to attract tourists to Crookston. Such a Bigfoot exhibit would cost approximately $10,000, the story read, and possible collaboration with the Polk County Historical Society and Crookston Area Chamber of Commerce would also be explored.

"The media wire services eventually picked up the Bigfoot story, and the rest, as they say, is history.

"To sum it up, in the next few weeks, hundreds of newspapers nationwide ran the story, and the executive director appeared live on dozens of radio shows across America. From Los Angeles to New York City, people wanted to know what was up with Bigfoot in Crookston.

"And that wasn't all. Television shows followed, and one in particular, 'Sightings' set up shop in the executive director's office to tape a segment for their show.

"It was Bigfoot mania in Crookston. Thousands of Baby Bigfoot dolls went on sale, and the annual Ox Cart Days parade featured two Bigfoot floats. A local gas station and convenience store sold bumper stickers that said: 'Crookston, Minnesota: The Bigfoot Capital of the World.'

"And one local eating establishment, RBJ's Family Restaurant, got in on the

fun with Bigfoot burgers and cookies, and even treated the crew from 'Sightings' to a Bigfoot feast after they were through shooting their Bigfootage.

"With all the attention, there was bound to be some controversy. Several city officials- claiming they were bombarded with outraged taxpayers demanding better use of their tax dollars- went public, assuring citizens that no public money would be spent on any Bigfoot project. A story appeared in the Times under the headline: 'Bigfoot: Big Scandal?'

"Slowly, however, the glare of the national spotlight dimmed. Radio stations and newspapers quit calling, hundreds of Baby Bigfoot dolls were shoved in store basements, and bumper stickers were peeled off cars. Kim Samuelson, owner of RBJ's Family Restaurant, still made Bigfoot cookies now and then, and customers could still enjoy a Bigfoot burger once a week. But until someone came forward with enough money to finance the construction of an actual Bigfoot replica, the phenomenon from the summer of 1995 was doomed to go down in history as a flash in the pan, Crookston's 15 minutes of fame, a joke told to grandchildren 50 years from now.

"That all changed..in May of 1996, when Samuelson herself put forth the money to have the nine-foot-tall, 300-pound replica constructed by a former taxidermist in Wisconsin.

"Bigfoot will call RBJ's home for the time being, but Samuelson's hope is that in the future, the portable replica will visit other spots in town and throughout the area.

"When he's not running with the moose east of town, Bigfoot has plenty of time for pictures, and he has a soft spot in his heart for kids.

"So take some shots, grab a bite to eat, and enjoy your time in Crookston:

The Bigfoot Capital of the World."

I rather had the impression that the city was coming at the

whole thing from the standpoint that Bigfoot was nothing but a legend to be used for attracting tourists, not a real animal. To underline that impression was a photo in the pamphlet showing a person in a very baggy-shaggy costume striding through some bushes, with the caption: "Pictured above is Crookston's famous roaming Bigfoot."

However, also in the pamphlet was one brief account of large footprints found in a cow pasture just north of a house near Gentilly Bridge on County Road 11 in the early spring of 1981. This sounded quite serious, so I decided it might be worth my time to go and check out this famous "Bigfoot Capital."

The imposing figure of Bigfoot stands just inside the entrance to RBJ's restaurant. Photos do not quite do it justice somehow, giving it a sort of "Harry and the Hendersons" type appearance. It is actually a very good likeness except for a bit too humanlike face, dark brown in color and very big. Previously it had been displayed outside. Now it stood next to a small display of three photos of the 1981 footprints, which were in snow and thus probably somewhat melted out if the time had been in the spring. The tracks seemed to have a convincing shape, however, with narrow heels and an indeterminate number of toes, looking somewhere in the neighborhood of 18 inches long (by my best guess) in comparison

to someone's foot in one picture. Apparently, there was no name to go with this

report; no one seemed to know where the pictures had come from, but they comprised the whole of known sasquatch activity around Crookston.

I spoke with Kim Samuelson, a friendly and bright young woman who said the

attitude behind the project was actually quite serious and that she thought there were probably still unknown things out in the world to be discovered. It was still her hope to expand the display in the future, assembling a whole information center about the creatures. She was surprised but interested to learn of the large number of reports on record from around the state, so I am hopeful that in the future, something constructive and accurate may still come about in Crookston.

CROOKSTON, MN - BIGFOOT CAPITAL OF THE WORLD

Bigfoot Creator: Curtis Christensen. Union Grove. Wl. The famous Crookston Bigfoot.

APPENDIX B

I t happens every time I attempt to put together a collection of reports like this- a few extra ones always come along after I think I'm finished and have to be tacked on at the end.

Ed Trimble heard recently of still more activity up in Clearwater County.

A young logger told of having seen strange tracks by a small, deep lake in the Buckboard Hills in mid-winter. Also, a sighting by a boy from the Tulaby Lake area is rumored. At the time of this writing, no further details are known, but Ed is trying to find out more.

It was also rumored that someone near Coon Rapids (which is ten to fifteen miles north of Minneapolis) had obtained clear videotape of a sasquatch. However, I do not trust the source I heard this from, and as I have heard nothing else about it from anywhere, I am inclined to reject this story.

And finally- this is not recent, but I couldn't include it in any other section- there is a particular investigator that I (and a number of others) are no longer on good terms with, but at one time, he was telling me what he had in his personal files for Minnesota, and the only thing I had not heard of before was the story of a man with initials R.R. who had had two separate experiences, an actual creature sighting several years ago and a track find in either 1990 or 1991. The investigator said he would get back to me with more details, but that was some years ago, and I don't even know where in Minnesota this is supposed to have happened in.

So, R.R., I can't use your full name here without permission, but if you know who you are and happen to read this, please contact me!

MINNESOTA SASQUATCH
BIBLIOGRAPHY

The following publications contain information on Minnesota sasquatch reports and/or the Minnesota Iceman.

BOOKS:

- Bord, Janet and Colin. "The Bigfoot Casebook," Harrisbura: Stackpole Books, 1982.
- Byrne, Peter. "The Search for Big Foot: Monster, Myth or Man?" Washington: Acropolis Books, 1975.
- Clark, Jerome and Loren Coleman. "Creatures of the Outer Edge," New York: Warner Books, 1978.
- Cohen, Daniel. "The Encyclopedia of Monsters," New York: Dodd, Mead & Co., 1982.
- "Monsters, Giants and Little Men from Mars: An Unnatural History of the Americas," New York: Dell Books, 1975.
- Gaffron, Norma. "Bigfoot: Opposing Viewpoints," San Diego: Greenhaven Press, 1989.

- Green, John. "The Sasquatch File," Agassiz: Cheam Publishing, 1973.
- "Sasquatch: The Apes Among Us," Victoria: Cheam Publishing, 1978.
- Guennette, Robert and Frances. "The Mysterious Monsters," Los Angeles: Sun Classic Pictures, 1975.
- Heuvelmans, Bernard and Boris Porshnev. "L'Homme de Neanderthal est Toujours Vivant," Paris: Librarie Plon, 1974.
- Krantz, Grover. "Big Footprints: A Scientific Inquiry into the Reality of Sasquatch," Boulder: Johnson Printing co., 1992.
- Napier, John. "Bigfoot: The Yeti and Sasquatch in Myth and Reality," New York: E. P. Dutton & Co., 1972.
- Norman, Eric. "The Abominable Snowmen," New York: Award Books, 1969.
- Perez, Danny. "Big Footnotes: A Comprehensive Bibliography Concerning Big- Foot, the Abominable Snowman and Related Beings," Norwalk: D. Perez Publishing, 1988.
- Place, Marion T. "Bigfoot All Over the Country," New York: Dodd, Mead & Co., 1978.
- Quast, Mike. "Creatures of the North: The New Minnesota Sasquatch Encounters," privately published, 1991.
- "The Sasquatch in Minnesota," privately published, 1990.
- Sanderson, Ivan T. "Things," New York: Pyramid Books, 1967.
- Scott, Beth and Michael Norman. "Haunted Heartland," New York: Warner Books, 1985.
- Smith, Warren. "Strange Abominable Snowmen," New York: Popular Library, 1970.
- Time-Life's "Mysteries of the Unknown- Mysterious Creatures," Alexandria: Time-Life Books, 1988.
- Wylie, Kenneth. "Bigfoot: A Personal Inquiry into a Phenomenon," New York: Viking Press, 1980.

MAGAZINE ARTICLES:

- Ayers, Bradley Earl- "The Thing that Stalks the Game Preserve," Fate, December, 1977.
- Hansen, Frank. "I Killed the Ape-Man Creature of Whiteface," Saga, July, 1970.
- INFO Journal, Vol. 3 No. 1, Autumn, 1972.
- "Mike Quast: On a Quest to Find Sasquatch," Minnesota Calls, November/Decem- ber, 1991 (plus a follow-up letter from Mike Quast in the following issue).
- Saga, June 6, 1969.
- Zeligman, Evelina. "The Puzzle of the 'Iceman,'" Asia and Africa Today, Jan- uary/February, 1983.

NEWSPAPER ARTICLES:

- Anderson, Jim. "Giant Footprint Signals a Time to Seek Strength," Red Wing Republican Eagle, July 23, 1988.
- Burford, Tom. "Clearwater County Man Says Tracks Made by Bigfoot- Did legendary creature leave its imprint in the snow in area near Long Lake Park?" Bagley Farmers Independent, March 27, 1991 (as well as follow-up articles by Tom Burford in the August 31, 1994 edition).
- Davey, Harry. "Sasquatch? There are 100s of them," Rainy River Reflections, International Falls Daily Journal, July 24, 1979.
- Dorn, Patrick. "Ice Creature Returneth!" Winona Daily News, May 13, 1983.
- Edstrom, Marv. "Litchfield Man Tracking Bigfoot," Wilmar West-Central Tribune, October 26, 1979.
- Freeberg, Ron. "Woman Claims Sighting Creature on Area Road," Rochester Post- bulletin, December 17, 1979.
- "He Won't Say what Made that Big Footprint," International Falls Daily Journal, September 14, 1979.

- "Man-Beast Sighted, Tracked Above Hovland," Cook County News Herald, April 1, 1991.
- Monsour, Theresa. "Edina Lads Determined to Track Down Bigfoot," St. Paul Pioneer Press, January 26, 1981.
- Okretich, Greg. "Unexplained Tracks Found by Local Resident," The Clearwater Review, March 20, 1991,
- Pantera, Tom. "Bigfoot Believer- Fargoan says he saw beast in Becker,"
- Fargo (ND) Forum, march 31, 1991 (about Mike Quast).
- Pumarlo, Jim. "Sasquatch Hunter Looks for the Beast in Koochiching County," International Falls Daily Journal, July 13, 1979.
- Quast, Mike. "Bigfoot Leads" (letter to the editor), Detroit Lakes Tribune, February, 1988.
- Reddin, Mike. "Police Probing Reported 'Animal' Attack," Fairmont Sentinel, November 27, 1978.
- "Strange Sightings in Clearwater County," Tri-County Canary, April 3, 1991. Wentzel, 8onnie. "Bigfoot... Myth or Reality?" Bemidji News Line, July 15, 1992.
- "White 'Creature' Sighted Near Tower," The Tower News, July 21, 1972.
- Yeager, Gordon. "'Ice Man' Not Real, but Murky Mystery is Left," Rochester Post-Bulletin, April 21, 1969.

ABOUT THE AUTHOR

Since sighting a sasquatch in Minnesota as a child, Mike Quast (right) has been extensively studying the subject and since 1987 has been actively on the trail of these animals in his home state of Minnesota. Born in 1967 in the town of Detroit Lakes, he now lives in Moorhead and is a graduate in Commercial Art from Northwest Technical College. He is the author of two previous books- "The Sasquatch in Minnesota" (1990) and "Creatures of the North: The New Minnesota Sasquatch Encounters" (1991)- and also co-editor of The Sasquatch Report newsletter.

To report sasquatch encounters or for more information, you can contact Mike at 1302 19 1/2 St. S. #20, Moorhead, MN 56560.

Encounters can also be reported to Tim Olson, also co-editor of The Sasquatch Report, at 1198 Oasis Street, Arcata, CA 95521-4430.

In the picture below, Tim visits the national monument at Crater Lake while on an expedition in southern Oregon.

Made in the USA
Monee, IL
15 September 2021

78095812R00154